Somerset Maugham

Anthony Curtis

Somerset Maugham

Macmillan Publishing Co., Inc.   New York

Macmillan Publishing Co., Inc.
866 Third Avenue, New York, N.Y. 10022

Library of Congress Cataloging in Publication Data

Curtis, Anthony.
    Somerset Maugham.

    1. Maugham, William Somerset, 1874–1965—Biography.
2. Authors, English—20th century—Biography.
PR6025.A86Z5718   823'.9'12   77-6618
ISBN 0-02-529280-3

First American Edition 1977

Printed in Great Britain

ILLUSTRATIONS
Page 1 The symbol warding off the evil
eye which was discovered by
Maugham's father in Morocco and used
by Maugham as a trade-mark on the
covers of all his books. This version of it
was designed by Graham Sutherland.

Page 2 Ronald Searle's caricature of
Somerset Maugham

Contents

Acknowledgments

The extract from *Prater Violet* by Christopher Isherwood is reproduced by kind permission of Eyre Methuen Ltd, London.

Photographs and illustrations were supplied by, or are reproduced by, kind permission of the following:

BBC: 189, 190
British Library: 2, 18, 52, 77, 97, 146, 151, 177
Camera Press, London: 131, 185, 193, 201, 205
City Museum, Stoke-on-Trent: 71
Courtesy of Lady Kelly (photo. Mander & Mitchenson): 68, 158 (left), 158 (bottom right)
Courtesy of the Rank Organization Limited (photo. Mander & Mitchenson): 186
Courtauld Institute of Art, London: 20–21
Crawford Municipal Art Gallery, Cork: 113
Douglas West Studios: 25
Emi-Pathé News: 143
Greater London Council (Print Collection): 51
Harvard University (photo. Angus McBean): 202
H. Andrew Freeth, R.A.: 167
Humanities Research Center, Texas: 158 (top right), 159 (left & right)
Jerry Bauer: 198
King's School, Canterbury: 28, 32, 34, 36–7
Kobal Collection, London: 179
Law Society: 17
Mander & Mitchenson Theatre Collection: 63, 75, 79, 81, 88, 90, 103, 118, 122, 123, 124, 125, 128
Mansell Collection, London: 140 (right), 141 (right), 152, 155
Mary Evans Picture Library, London: 120
National Portrait Gallery: 99 (above & below)

Popperfoto: 61, 100–1, 105, 140 (left), 141 (left), 187
Private Collection: 176
Radio Times Hulton Picture Library, London: 31, 39, 42, 49, 55,
    70, 85, 89, 93, 110, 110 (inset), 114, 115, 183
Roger Viollet, Paris: 15, 104
Sotheby & Co: 107, 136, 137
St Thomas's Hospital Archives/Greater London Record Office: 46–
    7, 53
Syndication International: 108, 135, 180, 192, 194, 195, 196, 197
Twentieth Century-Fox Film Company (photo. Mander & Mit-
    chenson): 171
United Press International, New York: 111
Weidenfeld and Nicolson Archives: 92

Picture Research by Philippa Lewis

All possible care has been taken in tracing the ownership of copy-
right material used in this book and in making acknowledgement for
its use.
If any owner has not been acknowledged the publishers apologize
and will be glad of the opportunity to rectify the error.

John's and Jill's

The cigar somehow completed Chatsworth. As he puffed it, he
seemed to grow larger than life-size. His pale eyes shone with a
prophetic light.

'For years I've had one great ambition. You'll laugh at me.
Everybody does. They say I'm crazy. But I don't care.'

He paused. Then announced solemnly: 'Tosca. With Garbo.'

Bergmann turned, and gave me a rapid, enigmatic glance. Then
he exhaled, with such force that Chatworth's cigar smoke was
blown back around his head. Chatsworth looked pleased. Evidently
this was the right kind of reaction.

'Without music, of course. I'd do it absolutely straight.' He
paused again, apparently waiting for our protest. There was none.

'It's one of the greatest stories in the world. People don't realise
that. Christ, it's magnificent.'

Another impressive pause.

'And do you know who I want to write it?' Chatsworth prepared
us for the biggest shock of all.

Silence.

'Somerset Maugham.'

Utter silence broken only by Bergmann's breathing.

Chatsworth sat back, with the air of a man who makes his
ultimatum. 'If I can't get Maugham, I won't do it at all.'

'Have you asked him?' I wanted to inquire, but the question
seemed unworthy of the occasion. I met Chatsworth's solemn eye,
and forced a weak nervous smile.

However, the smile seemed to please Chatsworth. He
interpreted it in his own way, and unexpectedly beamed back at
me.

'I bet I know what Isherwood's thinking,' he told Bergmann.
'He's right, too, blast him. I quite admit it. I'm a bloody
intellectual snob.'

From *Prater Violet* by Christopher Isherwood

Foreword

The legend of the sorcerer's apprentice, memorably set to music by Paul Dukas, presents a picture of youthful incompetence. The apprentice is given the humble task by the master of scrubbing the workshop clean. While the master is away the apprentice is tempted to try and use the sacred magic to save himself effort. Once under the spell the apparatus manifests an autonomy which the apprentice discovers he is powerless to resist. Only the timely return of the master prevents the premises from becoming overwhelmed by the elements.

Anyone who has ever tried to use words creatively will be familiar with the lesson of this cautionary tale. How rapidly they get out of control, multiplying themselves like the bewitched broomstick, threatening to swamp the original conception in banality and cliché. Then perhaps in despair at the mess we are making of it we pick up a story by Somerset Maugham and how easy it all seems. Here the tools used are as everyday, as ordinary, as the sorcerer's broomstick, but because they are reduced to a condition of complete obedience to the master's will, and made to serve his intention perfectly, they possess uncommon magic. The ordinary and the commonplace are raised to a level where they become charged with uncommon significance.

Maugham believed in both the magic and the effort; better than anyone he knew that the path to the former was only through the latter. As a writer he was both the sorcerer and the apprentice. He hated the notion of any kind of biography whether official or unofficial that would pry into the sources of his magic. He took legal measures during his life to prevent such a biography from ever appearing. It is not my intention here to try and defeat that embargo. On the other hand, Maugham did in the course of his work reveal a great deal about himself, not just in fictional guise but factually in prefaces, introductions, autobiographical essays and books. Even the notorious *Looking Back*, which appeared in *Show* magazine and *The Sunday Express* in 1962, when not making the unwarranted attack on the woman he married, which so deeply shocked both his intimate friends and his admirers throughout the world, did contain fascinating new information of a perfectly harmless nature about his childhood, his work as a secret agent, his relations with Churchill and so on. Since then a great deal has appeared about him in print by people who claim to have known him well.

It seems to me that the reader who has enjoyed Maugham's work over the years is entitled to know in general terms where the fact ends and the fiction begins, and that out of all this confusing mass of material a broad-brush portrait of the writer and his world might be attempted. I like to think that Maugham himself would have approved of the operation. At least I am only doing for him what he did for Jane Austen, Dickens, Flaubert, Melville, Tolstoy and others in that most readable book *Ten Novels and Their Authors*. In the wake of a centenary critical study *The Pattern of Maugham* (1974), and of the portrait I compiled, *The Faces of Maugham*, which was broadcast in that year on BBC Radio 3, I talked about Maugham to several of his friends and colleagues and felt I had acquired a deeper understanding of his personality which I have tried now to communicate to the reader with the aid of period illustrations.

I am indebted to the authors of all the books I mention in the text and also the labours of my picture researcher, Phillipa Lewis, and to the editor of the book at Weidenfeld and Nicolson, Hilary Arnold. Any errors of fact or taste are however my responsibility alone. Above all I am indebted to my brother, John Curtis of Weidenfeld, for first suggesting the project and for his persistent encouragement while it was in progress. I should like to thank, too, the former Headmaster of The King's School, Canterbury, Canon J.P. Newell for inviting me to give a King's Week lecture in 1974 on their eminent OKS in which I first had the chance to adumbrate some of the ideas in this book.

A.C.

1

From Embassy to Vicarage

The stately building in the Faubourg St Honoré, which housed the confinement of Edith Maugham when she gave birth to her fourth son on 25 January 1874, was once the residence of Napoleon's sister Pauline. Since 1814, when it was taken over by the Duke of Wellington, it had been the British Embassy. Edith's husband Robert Ormond Maugham, to whom she had been married for more than a decade, was the senior partner in the firm Maugham et Dixon, jurisconsultes anglais, whose Paris office was at 54 Faubourg St Honoré, almost opposite the road from the Embassy, and whose business largely consisted of handling the legal side of its affairs.

The Maughams did not normally stay in the Embassy; they had an agreeable apartment near the Rond Point at 25 Avenue d'Antin, as the street was then named. The reason for the removal of Edith there for the birth came about through a quirk of history. At the height of the Franco-Prussian war legislation had been put in train declaring that all boys born in France of foreign parents were French, in order that they should do military service. As Cynthia Gladwyn explains in *The Paris Embassy*, the law was never finally passed but while it was threatened the second floor of the Embassy was turned into a maternity ward so that the children who entered the world there would do so on British territory.

Three births have been traced there, all in 1874. Two were girls: one Violet Williams-Freeman, daughter of the second secretary, and the other Emily Lytton. The third child, Edith's son, was christened William Somerset Maugham. His middle name was derived from a remote military ancestor and he would wince in later years if anyone made the mistake of using it to his face. To family and friends he was always known as Willie.

In various ways Willie was a late arrival, and this did much to form his temperament. The privileged, abundant style of life which the Maughams and their circle enjoyed did not survive the war unscathed; the clientèle of the law practice shrank, money was harder to earn and memories of fleeing from a besieged Paris and the bloody horrors of the Commune were uncomfortably close. The social round pursued by the Maughams and other expatriates was resumed with as determined a gaiety as hitherto, but from time to time anxious glances might be discerned in the eyes of the hostess and guests.

A more immediate cause for anxiety in the circle was Mrs Maugham's health. She was the victim of tuberculosis of the lungs, as great a danger then as cancer is today. It had killed her own sister in 1869 when she was twenty-seven, and it was to afflict Willie when he was first married. The disease's way of striking at a beautiful young woman and cutting her off in her prime was not, unfortunately, confined to the romantic stage of Dumas *fils* and Verdi.

Moreover Willie was a late arrival within his own family. Nearly ten years separated him from his oldest brother, Charles Ormond, born in 1865, eight from Frederic Herbert, 'Freddie', the next oldest, and six from Henry Neville, 'Harry'. Had the fifth son, who died in infancy a few weeks before his mother, survived, Willie's attitude to his siblings might have been different and his whole outlook less competitive. As it was he inevitably had a very close relationship with his mother for the years they were together and a correspondingly traumatic sense of disruption after her death.

The métier of the Maughams was law. It was through the practice of English law that the family had risen to the eminence it enjoyed when Willie was born. In his own generation it rose further through the law when his brother Freddie was made Lord Chancellor of England and elevated to the peerage. In the first chapter of his novel *Christmas Holiday* Somerset Maugham described how a typical English family, the Masons, whose founder was a market gardener, scaled all the social heights until its head had become a pillar of the establishment. The origin of the Maughams lay likewise among the yeomanry of rural England and it was the nineteenth century that saw the consolidation of the family's position as gentry and the unmistakable evidence among its members of ability and leadership.

Somerset Maugham's nephew, Robin (the present Lord Maugham), in whom the Maugham literary genes have made a fresh manifestation, has traced the ramifications of this rise in his book, *Somerset and all the Maughams*. He uncovers the rural roots of the Maughams in the soil of Lincolnshire and Westmorland. A William

Maugham who farmed in that county in the eighteenth century had
a son William who became a clergyman and master of the Free
Grammar School at Stamford, and by his second wife a son Robert
who became a glazier.

It was this Robert Maugham who was Willie's great-great-grand-
father. He had a son William, born at Appleby in 1759, who
migrated to London and lived in the region of Chancery Lane,
where he seems to have earned his livelihood by serving the law
in some modest way, perhaps as a clerk. It is his son Robert, born
in London in 1778 and educated at Appleby Grammar School, in
whom we find the first striking incarnation of the Maugham genes.
He became a respected member of the legal profession and helped
to found the Law Society in 1832. He was its first secretary and
there is a portrait of him in its building in Chancery Lane. His career
rates a whole article in the *Law Society Gazette* and it is clear that
like his more famous grandson he was always ready to drive his pen
across the blank page, mainly on subjects connected with his profession, but also occasionally on more general topics, such as the
behaviour appropriate to a gentleman.

This lawyer possessed not just a disciplined mind and ambitious
power of application but also characteristic Maugham qualities of
physique and temperament. He was a small, dark, striking-looking
man with fine piercing eyes who seems at times to have had fits
of irascibility. Maugham repeats the story told by one of his father's
colleagues of how on observing a plate of baked potatoes being
carried in for lunch one day in his chambers he threw them in
disgust one by one at the wall.

His son, Robert Ormond Maugham, born 1832, was Willie's
father. With his large, sallow face he resembled him physically and
when he married at the age of thirty-nine the beautiful Edith Snell,
sixteen years his junior, there were malicious cracks in the
Maugham circle about Beauty and the Beast. However, he was a man
who inspired great affection not only in his wife and family but also
among the English children who came to play with his son. One
of these was Violet Freeman, later to become well known to literary
men as Mrs Violet Hammersley. She tells us that when Willie's
father 'took me on his knee to blow his watch open I remember
stealing over me a sense of complete safety and happiness'. As for
Willie himself in those days, Mrs Hammersley recalled an imaginative little boy, a natural leader of the group, who invented what
games they should play, and who would shock them by passing off

Robert Maugham, the writer's
grandfather whose portrait hangs in the
Law Society, which he helped to found.

counterfeit *sous* in exchange for sweets from the stall-holders of the
bois.

From his tenderest years Willie was an entertainer who aroused
a mixed response in his audience. But for all the legal ability of his
Maugham forebears, it may seem a far cry from their gift to his
own powers as an enchanter and spell-binder. Is there nothing in
the genes to suggest a strain of pure story-telling? Let us turn to
the background provided by his beautiful and popular mother. 'Mrs
Maugham,' Violet Hammersley remembered, 'was lovely, with rus-
set hair, brown eyes and creamy complexion and there was an air
of romance and tragedy about her.' She came of Cornish stock
tinged with blue blood on her mother's side that went back to the
time of the Norman Conquest. Edith Maugham was the second
daughter of a Major Charles Snell and his wife Anne Alicia. The

Edith Maugham, Willie's mother.

Major served in India where his daughter was born in 1840. As with Maugham's own parents there was a discrepancy in age between the couple and when the major died at fifty his wife was only twenty-four. She eventually returned to Europe to settle in Paris with her daughters where she and her youngest daughter Rose embarked upon a career of writing. They wrote novels for children in French. Mrs Snell wrote twelve novels and Rose six. It was a remarkable achievement for the widow to have turned herself into a successful author in an adopted language, and we may see in it anticipations of Maugham's power of directing his inspiration to the requirements of a specific market.

Maugham's inheritance was therefore propitious for the profession he finally chose, and so too was his environment at this time. Although he grew up as a small child mainly in the care of his French nurse with whom he shared a bedroom, only being permitted to see his mother for a few minutes after breakfast, he did none the less have opportunities to observe the adult world at its most fashionable and elegantly picturesque. One of his mother's greatest friends was Lady Anglesey, a striking American woman who had previously been married to Lord Kimberly. She possessed both the candour and the generosity of her race and when Willie was seven she presented him with a twenty-franc piece as a birthday present. In his eighties Maugham still treasured the memory of this windfall. When he was asked at the time how he wanted to spend it he replied that he wanted to go and see Sarah Bernhardt. The precocious request was granted and he went to the theatre for the first time in his life to see her in *Nana Sahib*. 'It was,' he wrote, 'an atrocious melodrama by Sardou. To me it was wonderfully thrilling.' This early passion for theatre had to wait until his student days for its fulfilment. When he returned to Paris in his youth he would go to the theatre, sometimes in the company of Harold Acton, who remembers how rapidly and accurately Maugham could predict how the plot of a play was going to develop, and how if it became too obvious he would leave before the end.

In common with other Parisians the English colony abandoned the city after the fourteenth of July. In Maugham's childhood the smart resort on which the *haut monde* descended was Trouville. The Maughams used to go to the then less modish Deauville where they rented a house. Mrs Maugham stayed for the season with her four sons and was joined by her husband at the weekend. It was a leisurely summer idyll, the scene painted often by Boudin with ladies

'View of Deauville' by Boudin the resort where the Maughams spent their summer holidays.

in long voluminous dresses sauntering by the sea, clasping their parasols and chatting idly. On one occasion one of the ladies was Lily Langtry, the royal paramour: Mrs Maugham turned her head away sharply as this immoral creature came into view.

In *Looking Back* Maugham gave the impression that the shabbily dressed painter plying his talent for hire along the beach, showing his work to these ladies, who would smile patronizingly, was in fact Boudin. Well at some time in his life Boudin may have had to resort to such tactics, but certainly not at any period that Maugham could actually remember. When Maugham was one year old Boudin was getting his first pictures accepted by the Salon, when Maugham was three he was getting prices varying from eighty-five to four hundred francs for a canvas (a lot of money in those days). In 1880, when Maugham was four, Boudin sold his picture *The Port of Trouville* for a record nine hundred francs. After that Boudin was taken up by the dealer Durand-Ruel who henceforth marketed his work for him, and you would have been as likely to pick up a Boudin on the plage at Trouville for a few francs as you would have been to pick up an Edward Seago for a fiver on the beach at Bournemouth in the 1960s. I mention this merely to show how cautious one must be in taking Maugham's anecdotes as historical truth.

Boudin or not, what childhood could be more blissful, more privileged, more 'normal'? This happy state was not to last very long. When Maugham was nearly seven Edith became pregnant for the sixth time; medical opinion inclined to the view that pregnancy was good for consumption. One day she was well enough to have herself photographed. Maugham kept her portrait in his bedroom until the day he died.

The day before Willie's birthday in 1882 Edith gave birth to another son, Edward Alan. The baby died the next day on Maugham's eighth birthday. Six days later Mrs Maugham died at the age of forty-one. No reader of *Of Human Bondage* will need reminding of the intensity of his grief. His sense of isolation was exacerbated by the fact that his older brothers were now all away from home at boarding school in England and his own education was in the hands of an English clergyman in Paris who had the task of instructing him in his own native language, which at this time Maugham spoke a good deal less fluently than he did French.

After his mother's death Willie remained in Paris in the charge of his nurse whose affection provided him with a substitute for his mother. His father's legal labours did not leave him all that much time to lavish on his son. Robert was putting into effect a grandiose plan for building a house that they could live in during the summer out at Suresnes on the top of a hill with a view of Paris in the distance. It was a pardonable folly designed to resemble a house on the Bosporus. Willie and his father used to go down the Seine on Sundays by *bateau-mouche* to see how it was getting on. When it was finally completed Robert Maugham had engraved upon its windows a sign against the evil eye that he had discovered in Morocco. But for him the sign did not possess its desired power. He was destined never to enjoy the view from his property. When it was all ready for occupation in 1884 Robert Maugham died, at the age of sixty. He left Willie in the care of an uncle, a Church of England parson in Whitstable, the seaside town near Canterbury in Kent.

Maugham's childhood in the Whitstable and Canterbury of the 1880s is familiar to his admirers through two novels, *Of Human Bondage* and *Cakes and Ale*. Throughout his career Maugham drew very heavily as a novelist on his memories of what he had actually observed. He used people, surnames, architecture, landscape, incident and anecdote with a disregard for defamation curious in the son of a lawyer and never more so than in these two books. Undoubtedly we do learn a great deal that is literally true about his life in the vicarage with his uncle and aunt from reading them. But it is important to remember that they are works of fiction, and that whatever close correspondences there may be between Whitstable and Blackstable, the latter was the invention of Somerset Maugham.

In his old age Maugham wrote an essay on Dickens in which he refers to the famous episode where Dickens was sent as a child to work in a relative's blacking warehouse at Hungerford Stairs, a time Dickens found intolerably painful to recall in later life. Maugham comments:

As his imagination went to work on his recollections, he was filled, I suspect, with pity for the little boy he had been; he gave him the pain, the disgust, the mortification which he thought he, famous, affluent, beloved, would have felt if he had been in that little boy's place. And seeing it all so vividly, his generous heart bled, his eyes were dim with tears, as he wrote of the poor lad's loneliness and misery at being betrayed by those in whom he had put his trust. I do not think he consciously exaggerated; he couldn't help exaggerating his talent, his genius if you like was based upon exaggeration.

... as is that of any novelist, especially Maugham, those very shrewd observations apply with as great a force to the writer of them as to their subject. For one thing there is a discrepancy of mood between the two novels encompassing Maugham's childhood. In *Bondage* all is gloom and doom, Blackstable appears as a prison from which the orphan escapes only into the larger hell of Tercanbury; in *Cakes and Ale* Blackstable is a quaintly congenial place for a lad with the bonus of a friendly bunch of outsiders with whom to roister and explore the surrounding countryside by bicycle.

Both books are true. Childhood does consist of alternating moods of elation and despair, and we may be sure that for all their richness of recall both books leave out a good deal. Willie undoubtedly was in a situation of great isolation and wholly dependant upon the will of his uncle and his aunt for his well-being. Time was to prove that his will was equal to theirs and, ultimately, stronger, but for the moment the outlook was pretty bleak. Robert had not left a vast fortune, only £4,690 18s 6d to be divided among his four sons which when it was invested meant that they would each have an income of £150 a year. Clearly, said his uncle, delivering the first major blow to Willie's morale, they could not afford to employ the nurse with whom he had journeyed across the Channel. She was sent back to France. It was a bitter lesson in the meaning of economic dependence. Other lessons, large and small, followed rapidly. One of the most vivid came when the Vicar sat down to eat his egg before taking the evening service. He sliced the top off it and handed this section to Willie as his portion. After the easy and plentiful life of the apartment in the Avenue d'Antin these little acts of parsimony did more than anything to make the boy feel humiliatingly disoriented and alien to his new environment. The outward and audible sign of this alienation was his stammer; it was a pretty bad one and remained with Maugham for the rest of his life. Its effect on the child was to prevent his speech from keeping up with the precocious rapidity of his mind. There could hardly be a stronger stimulus to turn to writing as a source of self-expression than this.

One photograph survives showing Willie with his uncle against the background of the Old Vicarage at Whitstable. They are holding hands on the lawn on what appears to be a balmy summer day but the shot is too distant for one to make out the expression on their faces. It is like a scene at the opening of a film before the camera zooms forward to bring the two antagonists into close-up. What one can discern is the contrast in height, and the fact that both of them appear to be in their Sunday best, the High Church Vicar in his

The Vicarage, Whitstable, where Willie lived when a schoolboy. It was demolished in 1972/3.

full clerical habit with swirling skirts and conical hat. Presumably it was a Sunday and they were about to go to the parish church which was two miles away at the other end of the town. The stretch of field between, Maugham would come to know extremely well.

Henry Macdonald Maugham was the only surviving brother of Robert. He was educated at London University and Oriel College, Oxford, and had been the incumbent of various livings before he was made Vicar of Whitstable in 1871, around the time the Vicarage was built. In 1858 he had married a German woman of thirty whom he appears to have met in England, Barbara Sophia von Scheidlen, daughter of a Nuremberg banker and merchant. The couple remained childless and by the time of Willie's arrival they were well into middle age. In spite of their parsimony they employed two maids and other servants at the Vicarage, domestic labour being very cheap at this time because unemployment among working-people was very high.

Parson Maugham inherited the deep-set eyes and strong face of his forebears, setting it off with a long curving moustache; his wife had the plaited crown of a lady from the continent above her pudgy features and tightly buttoned dress. It would be an agreeable coup if one were able to discover that 'old Maugham', as he was known locally, had been seriously maligned by his nephew's great novel, and that there was an unexpectedly benign and human side to him. But if this is so it has been astonishingly well concealed over the years and the portrait we have of him as the Reverend Carey must stand as the definitive one. A slightly more detached first-hand observer than Willie, his nephew Freddie, said of him: 'I am afraid he was very narrow-minded and a far from intelligent cleric. And I cannot truthfully praise him as a guardian of boys.'

Still, there must have been redeeming moments of pure pleasure and escape in that childhood. When he was in his seventies on a visit to Canterbury Maugham returned to the Vicarage (which has since then, alas, been pulled down); he went into the dining-room and he wrote inside a copy of his own *Notebook* published a few years before: 'I write this in the dining-room of the Old Vicarage at Whitstable where I spent all my holidays when I was at school. In this room I had my first lessons at whist ...' Surely this inscription implies some lighthearted evenings when the Vicar, Sophie and little Willie shuffled the pack and, in that deep competitive silence which descends upon the family circle at such a time, enjoyed the rigour of the game? Maugham's love of card-games – later in life it was to be bridge, patience and backgammon – began here.

But what does he mean when he says that he spent 'all my holidays' in the dining-room? What was he doing there? Reading. His own bedroom upstairs was tiny, the study where the fire smoked was sacred to the Vicar, the drawing-room was too grand and august, and so when the remains of the meal had been cleared away by the maids the little boy had the dining-room all to himself. And there like Jane Eyre and other nineteenth-century orphans, he would curl up with a book and for long satisfying hours he would banish present miseries through a sustained use of the imagination.

One fact about Parson Maugham – vain, bigoted, selfish, lazy, inflexible – and all the negative characteristics we now associate with him – has not been sufficiently emphasized: he was a great collector of books. He may not actually have read many of them but he did acquire them from the secondhand bookshops in Whitstable and Canterbury and put them on the shelves of his study. His nephew had the freedom of those shelves, and to be left alone in a house full of books is no bad beginning for a writer. In those days books were plentifully illustrated by steel engravings and Willie would feast his eyes upon pictures of mosques and minarets, palaces and terraces, pillars and grottoes as he perused the memoirs of travellers in the East. His greatest find was the standard translation by Lane Poole of the *Thousand and One Nights* which he devoured; then there were Scott's Waverley Novels to be got through, Lewis Carroll and many more ephemeral works of fiction. Somewhere on those shelves there was a scientific work that when published in 1857 had created a great flurry in the clerical dovecotes, Darwin's *Origin of Species*, which he would also read with absorption when he was older. But for the moment it was the soothing, healing balm of story and romance that captivated him.

The immediate problem was where he should go to school and the choice fell on The King's School, Canterbury, conveniently closer than Dover College, where his brothers had been sent. But he was not yet quite ready for it, so for a while his education proceeded under the supervision of his uncle and aunt, whose world was narrowly restrictive, governed by astonishingly powerful taboos and conventions – in its way a microcosm of late Victorian England. Whitstable was not then the popular holiday resort it was later to become. It was a self-contained little town dependent for its prosperity on the oyster farms and colliers that brought their cargoes to its bay. Its inhabitants belonged to the Kentish families who had lived there for generations, people like the Ganns and the Kemps, leading a settled, parochial life. They were units in a social structure that had two main axes: class and creed. If you were church like Parson Maugham and his flock, you did not consort with chapel folk, and if you were gentry, as the Maughams were just, you naturally kept a proper distance between yourself and the local tradesman, not to mention the lower rung of fishermen, artisans, servants and other working-persons.

When Sophie Maugham walked down the High Street with little Willie to do her shopping she averted her eyes if the Dissenting Minister or his wife came by, with as great a coolness as Edith Maugham turning away from the sight of Lily Langtry on the promenade at Deauville. The shops she patronized for her provisions were inevitably those whose proprietors worshipped in her husband's church. Unfortunately church was outnumbered by the opposition on the basis of two to one, and the chapels were more conveniently sited in the centre of the village, all of which made the custom of

Willie aged ten, when a pupil at the junior school of The King's School, Canterbury.

the Vicar's wife a delicate matter of bargaining and diplomacy.

As he tagged along in the wake of his aunt Willie registered indelible impressions of these people. One of the most memorable was Sibert Saunders, the bank manager of Hammond and Co's bank, and his uncle's churchwarden whom he immortalized in *Of Human Bondage* as Josiah Graves. Sophie was in the habit of concluding her shopping by a gossip with his sister in the airless front parlour above the bank on such Cranford-like topics as the new bonnet of Mrs Wilson, the wife of 'the richest man in Blackstable ... thought to have at least five hundred a year, and he had married his cook' – in reality a Mrs George Holden, married to Whitstable's leading capitalist and shipowner. After this respite they would resume shopping and then perhaps go down one of the sidestreets, where fishermen were mending their nets, to gaze for a moment or two at the sea before returning to the Vicarage. It was a monotonous routine but a safe one; as an appendage of his aunt Willie had a status of a kind and security. But soon the moment arrived for him to leave Whitstable in the term time and go to nearby Canterbury as a pupil at The King's School united by long tradition to the Cathedral. There for the first time in his life he would be entirely on his own.

2

The Black Book and Ibsen

Maugham joined the Junior Department of The King's School, Canterbury, in September 1884 when he was ten. The Vicar took him by train from Whitstable to the West Station and in a fly to the red-brick building in Palace Street. Shades of the prison-house closed upon the growing boy. 'Tell him I stammer, Uncle,' he urged as they were ushered into the presence of the Headmaster. The breezy manner of this pedagogue, the Reverend George Blore (Mr Watson in *Bondage*) did nothing to reassure his tongue-tied new pupil. Blore was a gigantic figure of a man who soon passed Willie over to another pupil to be shown round, and Willie went through that agony of apprehension which anyone who has ever been to an English prep school experiences but which most people are content to forget.

The King's School had over a hundred day-pupils, several of whom lived as far away as Whitstable or further, but Maugham became a boarder straight off. No doubt the Vicar was glad to be free of his presence during the term. Sophie, who had become fond of her nephew and who did not have long to live, may have regretted losing him. Nowadays the shock of the break with the home environment which boarding-school education administers to a young boy is tempered by understanding teachers, but in Maugham's time prep school was harsh and often cruel. The method proceeds in a curious way. By throwing a child into the constant companionship of his contemporaries, his 'peer-group' in modern jargon, he becomes at first acutely conscious of his own character, the defects of which (if that is the right word) are mercilessly high-lighted for him within the group. Gradually, though, he identifies with the prevailing mystique of the school and shedding his self-consciousness discovers his own personality as a member of a highly competitive but also companionable community. That at any rate is the theory. But with Willie Maugham it did not work: the sense of separateness remained

strong and intractable even after he had gained a measure of acceptance and considerable academic success.

Naturally the stammer was a source of teasing but slightly less
of a disability at school than the club-foot Maugham wished upon
his hero Philip Carey. The precise sympton is not really important;
what matters is the chronic self-consciousness which it epitomized.
Even the happiest childhoods are full of injustices but little Willie
never seems to have been able, as we say, to let go and suffer his
situation cheerfully, as most children learn to do. The precocious

gaze of the future novelist was always uncovering the sore places, refusing to allow wounds to heal; meantime stabs of insight into the completeness of his dependence created new gashes in the psyche.

If Whitstable was teeming with petty snobberies and cramping social distinctions, Canterbury was imprisoned in them on an even grander scale. But whereas in Whitstable he was a privileged observer of the system, here in the school he was a part of it, vulnerable to a lashing from the tongue or cane of any master whose path he crossed and the taunts and bullying of any more powerful boy. Of course he was teased and bullied. Of course his stammer was held up to ridicule. Children left on their own can be as lacking in decent human feeling as guards in a concentration camp. But I doubt that he was teased or bullied excessively. My impression is that he had a much less wretched time than, say, C.S. Lewis in his year at Malvern or Cyril Connolly as a Lower Boy at Eton. There

A page from the Black Book in which the misdemeanours of pupils at The King's School were recorded.

is no evidence that Maugham was ever caned, although his name is on record as appearing in the school's Black Book in which pupils misdemeanours were recorded. Maugham's offence is listed there as 'inattention', the one crime in after-life of which he was never guilty.

Even so let us freely admit that here was stony ground upon which to be stranded for such a sensitive soul. The masters whose nick-names have survived, Sighs, Tar, Winks, Squirts and Pat, sound a miserable crew. 'Tar', for instance, the Reverend L.G.H. Mason, who taught Latin and recited Browning with gusto, took especial delight in ridiculing a boy in front of his class-mates through wither-ing bursts of sarcasm. Like Tar the other masters were all clergy, and many of the boys clergymen's sons, who were themselves des-tined to devote their lives to the Church. Attendance at divine ser-vice in the Cathedral which the school adjoins formed a large part of the curriculum. Boys whose parents were not clergy came from the narrow range of gentlemanly professions, and the ideal of the reliable, selfless English gentleman, fit to form part of an élite that ruled a vast Empire, was instilled into them from their earliest years. Woe betide the boy whose background lay beyond the pale in trade or commerce.

Yet if one turns to the testimony of others who were at The King's School near to the time of Maugham it does not seem to be quite such a terrible place: purgatorial shall we say, rather than positively hellish? For the moment there was no possibility of escape. Willie tackled the curriculum of the Junior School, containing much Latin, with the same formidable power of application that he later gave to any intellectual or creative task set before him. He ceased gradually to be in awe of the Head and his contemporaries, and he won several academic prizes ('worthless books', he said, 'on bad paper, but in gorgeous bindings decorated with the arms of the school') rising eventually to the position of head boy and winning a scholarship to the main school at the age of thirteen. This per-mitted him to wear a short black gown over his Eton collar and jacket.

Then it all began again. Once more he was the lowest of the low and had to suffer the verbal whips and scorns of the teaching staff. He never forgot the moment when he suffered a total verbal paralysis while construing Latin in front of the irascible Reverend B.B. Gordon who yelled at him: 'Speak, you blockhead, speak!' Happily while he was there a new phase was beginning in the history

A group of masters at The King's
School in 1886 – *from left to right*
Mason, Price, Hodgson and Campbell.

of The King's School from which Maugham benefited. A Head-master was appointed of humble background and enlightened liberal views, to the consternation of Tar, Winks and Co, in the person of the Reverend Thomas Field (Mr Perkins in the novel). He brought a breath of modern languages and sciences, of sweetness and light to the old classical grind, and humane encouragement into his relations with a clever, difficult boy like Maugham. It was probably Field who showed Maugham a picture of the Acropolis and the Theatre of Dionysus, thus first opening his eyes to the civilized horizons to which his whole life would be so determinedly directed. It was through such kindnesses that the seeds were sown of the ultimate reconciliation between Maugham and The King's School brought to pass by Canon Shirley, after the Second World War. A school photograph of the 1880s shows Maugham sitting cross-legged at Field's feet.

More important than his relations with the masters were those with his fellow-pupils. He soon discovered where his real power lay – in the accuracy of his insights. If he suffered wounds he was also capable of inflicting them. His tongue was as sharp, if not sharper, than anyone's. On the whole he remained an outsider, a swot, a confirmed bookworm, but when he was old enough to share a study he formed the first of those relations, the beginning of that impulse to form possessive and exclusive attachments, that brought him so much misery in later life. We do not know who the boy was. In the novel he calls him Rose: it was a name he was to use again for the love-object in a Blackstable novel. Among his contemporaries there were two boys called Roe and one called Ross. It may have been one of them or it might have been a boy called Ashenden (another name he appropriated later on for a different purpose) or it might have been Hamilton or Donaldson or Robinson.

What mattered was not the name but the fact that this boy and Willie Maugham became close companions. For the first time in his life he knew the joy of shared experience instead of brooding in the angry, festering solitude of his own mind. The friendship flourished and the two boys became inseparable. When it was at its height with Maugham's emotional investment in it running dangerously high, he suffered a term's absence from school through an attack of pleurisy. He was sent to recuperate on the French Riviera to an English tutor's at Hyères. The interruption to the regular routine of the school year completely unsettled Maugham,

The fifth form at The King's School, 1899. Somerset Maugham, aged fifteen and wearing his scholar's gown, is sitting on a chair second from the right.

especially when on his return he discovered that 'Rose', whoever he was, though by no means unfriendly, no longer felt as strongly about Willie as he still did about him.

Here again Maugham was incapable of suffering the blow to his pride by shrugging it off. Instead he took it mortifyingly to heart and secretly decided to leave The King's School as soon as he could. He campaigned with his uncle to cut short his time there. It seemed a crazy idea because in spite of his somewhat delicate health, Maugham was one of the brightest boys of his year at Canterbury, doing very well in his work and an obvious candidate for a scholarship to Oxford or Cambridge. Both the Headmaster and the Vicar were utterly opposed to him leaving school prematurely. But they reckoned without the boy's cunning and persistence, helped by a further bout of illness and another term at Hyères. He enlisted the support of his aunt for his plan and she wrote to her German relations, one of whom wrote back to say that she knew of a lady in Heidelberg who was married to a professor at the university and who had students staying in her home *en pension*. After further correspondence and discussions with the Headmaster the Reverend Maugham somewhat surprisingly agreed that his nephew should leave Canterbury and continue his education in Germany.

In later life Maugham often said that he regretted not having sat his scholarship and gone to Cambridge like his brother Freddie. And in the novel there is a brilliant little scene where he shows how easily the Head could have drawn him back into the fold by a few honeyed words. But perhaps there is an unconscious wisdom in these matters, some *daimon* directing us away from the obvious course towards the one that is most appropriate for our particular needs. We may be sure that Oxford or Cambridge would have produced an impressive and successful W. Somerset Maugham, but the one who was to make a contribution to literature began to emerge at Heidelberg.

Maugham warmed from the first to the place with its ancient university, its tree-lined streets and its ruined *schloss*, from which one could observe the majestic sweep of the Rhine. He also found much to stimulate him in his encounters with the infinite variety of student and professorial life with which Heidelberg teemed at the end of the nineteenth century. One of the great recurring rhythms of Maugham's entire life, that of escaping abroad among unfamiliar surroundings for renewal and inspiration, had been set in motion.

Heidelberg University where Maugham
completed his formal education.

Maugham was now sixteen, and still very innocent. He had a
room in Frau von Grabau's pension, and £15 a month allowance
sent to him by his uncle, out of the money left by his father. Apart
from his landlady and her husband, who gave the young Englishman
instruction in German, the chief inmates of the *pension* consisted
of her two daughters who were older than Willie and a son who
was a year or so younger. Then there were the other students, all of
whom were several years older too; there was a Frenchman, a Chinese
and an American. Maugham made his first friendship with the last,
a New England classical scholar who taught Greek at Harvard and
had a taste for intellectual conversation especially about theology.
He appears as Weeks in *Bondage*. It was in discussions with him

that Maugham discovered how simplistic was the faith in which he had grown up and faced for the first time the problem of the huge variety of creeds that existed in the world all of whose adherents were convinced of their unique truth. This American took Maugham on holiday with him to Switzerland for two weeks, and lent him Renan's *Life of Jesus*. Though apparently a believer himself, he led Maugham towards agnosticism.

The American's influence was important and liberating but it took second place in his memories of this period to that of the student who succeeded the American after he had departed for Berlin. He was an Englishman of twenty-six called John Ellingham Brooks. He had been called to the Bar after leaving Cambridge but had given that up and was now preparing himself for the life of a poet. He had come to Heidelberg to learn German, and was a perfect specimen, given a few more inches, of the 'Dorian Gray' homosexual aesthete of the 1890s with his finely cut features, his curly hair through which he had a habit of running his hand, and his wistful expression. He appears in *Bondage* as Hayward and in *The Summing-Up* as Brown.

He first saw Maugham in the *pension* reading *Tom Jones*. Brooks told him patronizingly that there was no harm in Fielding, but he would be much better off reading Meredith's *Diana of the Crossways*. This advice started Maugham reading books far beyond the scope of anything he had heard mentioned at The King's School. Under Brooks's guidance Maugham absorbed the authors of the *fin-de-siècle* and faced the rarefied challenge of their values. He not

John Ellingham Brooks, an early influence on Maugham's literary development

only read the whole of Meredith but also Swinburne, Verlaine, Walter Pater, Newman, Arnold, and he studied Dante. Brooks had a particular enthusiasm for Fitzgerald's *Omar Khayyám*, then known only to a few, and would recite it. He had written out the quatrains in long-hand, printed copies being difficult to obtain.

It was heady stuff for an adolescent. Maugham was too inexperienced to see through a poseur who happened to possess a measure of taste. Whatever his later view of Brooks may have contained of scorn and contempt, he was grateful for the spark that set alight that catholic fire to consume and assimilate the best in literature which remained with him for the whole of his life.

Both 'Weeks' and Brooks were, it seems, homosexuals and they were, one must assume, attracted to the handsome stammering English boy. As Maugham later reflected, trips to the ruined castle with tea on the terrace, or to Konigsthal to see the view of the Neckar valley, were not taken solely for the pleasure of hearing the young man stutter out his callow opinions of Renan or Matthew Arnold. However nothing erotic came of it, he says. His public school education had left Maugham totally innocent in such matters and although sex was very much in the air in the *pension*, as far as the Frau Professor's daughters and the male lodgers were concerned, the notion of a sexual relationship between himself and a man had not yet consciously entered Maugham's mind.

The ninetyish Platonism of Brooks was an intellectual stimulus not the beginning of an erotic initiation. That would come in London and Italy later. As well as Brooks's recommendations of authors to read there were plenty of names being bandied about in the University where Maugham was preparing for his matriculation. In particular the great explosion of realistic drama, that had just begun to sweep across Europe, had made its mark upon Heidelberg to the disgust of the Frau's Professor husband. Maugham and Brooks visited the local theatre several times and they not only saw plays by Ibsen – Maugham once actually observed the great man himself drinking beer in a café in Munich – but also Sudermann's *Die Ehre* (Honour) with its clash of values between the workers and the bourgeoisie, and the plays of the mordant French writer, Henry Becque.

Apart from that infantile birthday visit to see Sarah Bernhardt Maugham up to this time had had no direct experience of theatre. The touring companies in the Whitstable Assembly Rooms were never patronized by his guardians. Now he could go to the theatre every night if he wished. All the awkwardness he felt disappeared once he sat in a darkened theatre. The claustrophobic world of Ibsen seemed more real than what up to now he had taken for reality. In the theatre at Heidelberg Maugham formed his life's ambition to write plays.

An equally momentous revolution was occurring in the opera-house through the music drama of Wagner who was a name to conjure with in the University. The Herr Professor regarded him, too, as a nine days' wonder. Music was the least important of the arts for Maugham, but he learnt now about Wagner and heard enough of his operas later to refer to them knowingly whenever he needed a musically-minded character in one of his stories. More to his taste was Goethe, part of his more formal studies, whose influence on him was lifelong. He also attended lectures by the star turn of the philosophy department, Kuno Fischer, who was giving lectures on Schopenhauer. Marvelling at their acrobatic virtuosity Maugham acquired a taste for metaphysical speculation which prompted him when he was an old and distinguished man, to write an essay on

Students at Heidelberg in a serious but convivial mood.

Kant and try to explain the intricacies and subtleties of his philosophy to his vast flock of readers. At Heidelberg Maugham was therefore a most eager apprentice of civilized learning: he never ceased to be such an apprentice until the day he died.

In the formal sense he ceased to be a student on his matriculation and returned home to Whitstable. Life went on there in the same rigid way but his aunt and uncle no longer seemed the formidable presences of his childhood; they appeared now old and sad. Yet the latter was still his guardian – along with a solicitor colleague of his father's, Albert Dixon – and the question had to be decided of what he was going to do. The idea of going to Cambridge cropped up again, to be dismissed once and for all. The Vicar wrote to an Oxford friend, now eminent in the Civil Service, to see if there was an opening there but nothing resulted. Meanwhile Dixon arranged for Maugham to have a trial run in the offices of a firm of chartered accountants. He went for a few weeks and absolutely hated it. He found more snobbery there than at any other time in his life. He returned to the Vicarage in disgust. He was not afforded a hero's welcome. It was the local doctor who finally emerged with the solution to the problem of Willie's future. Why not, he said, let him try medicine? The Vicar agreed, heartily glad of anything that would remove the tiresome problem of his nephew's choice of profession from his mind, and Willie agreed too, seeing that this would allow him to do what he now wanted more than anything else, to live in London. Once again he bade Sophie goodbye and went on his way. As for Sophie herself she died a year later in Germany in August 1892. Three years later, in his sixties, Parson Maugham married a Miss Ellen Mary Matthews who was a great contrast to his first wife. A general's daughter from Bath, she was an amateur painter and she liked a joke. By all accounts she and the Vicar were very happy.

3

In and Out of Medicine

'I do not know a better training for a writer,' Maugham wrote in *The Summing Up*, 'than to spend some years in the medical profession.' He spent five formative years of his youth in it from 1892, when he enrolled at St Thomas's, the teaching hospital in South London, to 1897. At the end of that period Maugham had qualified but he never actually practised as a doctor. It was never his intention to practise if he could avoid doing so. By the time he had started on his medical studies he was absolutely clear in his mind that what he wanted to be was a writer. Medicine was a cover behind which he could acquire the skills and knowledge needed for his real profession; it was also an exhaustingly acquired insurance policy against eventual failure. Maugham was very conscious of the need to earn a decent livelihood, and if literature let him down he reckoned he would always be able to get a job as a ship's doctor, combining work with his passion for travel.

And at the same time he determined to do all he could to see that literature did not let him down. He did not just dream about writing and put it off until he had the security of his medical qualifications, he actually started to write: he kept a notebook in which he jotted paradoxical observations about life in the style of Oscar Wilde, also longer character sketches of his friends and colleagues, plus some gems from his landlady's talk. He became very fond of her incidentally. In addition to all this jotting he wrote plays and short stories. The two earliest of his stories were 'Daisy' and 'A Bad Example', both of which he claims to have written when he was eighteen. They were later published in a volume of stories, *Orientations* (1899), his third book, never reprinted. Both contain fascinating intimations of things to come. 'Daisy' is set in Blackstable, the first mention of that place in print, and describes a local girl who goes, as it seems to Blackstable, to the bad. 'A Bad Example' is the story of a Cockney working-man who tries to follow Christ's

A ward at St Thomas's Hospital, where
Maugham studied medicine, in the
1890s.

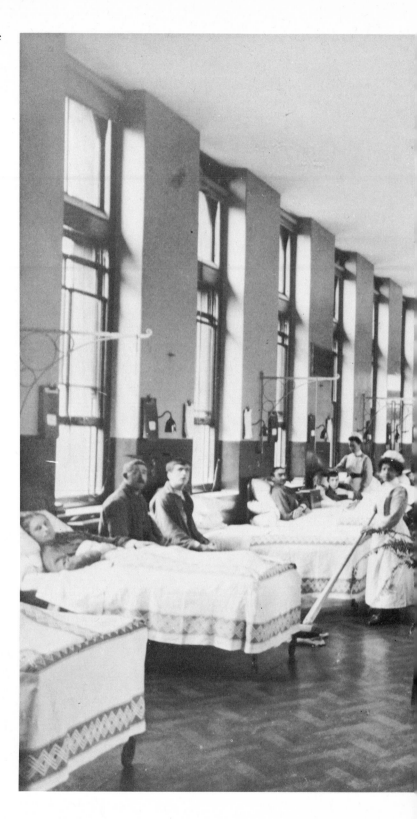

maxim by giving all he has to the poor to the disgust of his family, an idea Maugham used many years later in his last play, *Sheppey*.

While starting thus to write fiction seriously, Maugham set himself another long course of reading. He believed in preparing himself for his ultimate profession with the same thoroughness as for his immediate one. 'I was indeed the industrious apprentice,' he said. 'During the time I was at St Thomas's Hospital I went systematically through English, French, Italian and Latin literature.' If his initial approach to medicine had been rather lukewarm he soon became completely absorbed in it. The hospital provided him with the opportunity to observe some richly eccentric characters among the instructors and to make some friends among his fellow-students. Above all he learned to look upon the harsh facts of life, upon pain, bereavement and incurable disease with scientific detachment, an attitude that found its way into his writing.

The side of his work which most deeply impressed him was that of attending the women of Lambeth, whose slum dwellings lay close to the hospital, when they gave birth to their usually unwanted children. Down those mean, violent streets went young Mr Maugham, clutching his black doctor's bag, hot-foot to the confinement of some poor battered cow of a wife. During his obligatory stint of work as an obstetric clerk, Maugham attended sixty-three confinements in three weeks. In company with a professional midwife he would spend many hours of waiting in those squalid houses, where several large families might be occupying different floors, their members existing on a pittance which made his own small private income seem princely. His attentive writer's eyes, greedy for copy, took in every detail. At the same time he was impatient to make his name and had already started to approach publishers. He was attracted to T. Fisher Unwin, who was building up a list of contemporary fiction and had made a stir in the literary pond with a series of novels published under *noms-de-plume*. The series in lemon jackets was known as The Pseudonym Library. Part of their notoriety stemmed from the reader having to guess who the author really was. Maugham sent Fisher Unwin the two stories mentioned earlier in the hope that they might be suitable for the series. The publisher wrote back to say that unfortunately they were too short, but if Mr Maugham cared to send him a novel of the requisite length, short by ordinary novel standards, he would be happy to consider it.

This first tiny tug at Maugham's line was greatly encouraging.

The young author set to work at once to shape some of the material he had gathered while on his pregnancy rounds. He did not make the mistake of rendering the life of the London poor all gloom. Instead he invented a highly attractive heroine and showed her and her neighbours disporting themselves in the countryside on Bank holiday when not imprisoned in their grim street. With a touch of irony he called the story 'A Lambeth Idyll' and the pseudonym he chose was 'William Somerset'. When he was under the influence of Ellingham Brooks's fastidious taste, Maugham aspired to write in the ornate manner of the *fin-de-siècle*, but now in his first book he turned to a style of writing which aimed to be naturalistic. He strove to reproduce external objects and settings exactly as the eye perceived them and to render the rough Cockney speech of his characters, with its rapidity of repartee, exactly as the ear heard it.

Far from wishing to retreat in horror from the squalor and ugliness of real life into a dream of beauty and order begotten by art, Maugham joined those writers of the nineteenth century who tried to depict the squalor and ugliness as vividly and as accurately as possible. In making this effort Maugham discovered his true style, a deceptively simple way of writing that sometimes seems to totter perilously close to banality, which served him so well over such a long and fruitful literary life. The style derived from two currently fashionable movements, one French and the other English. Maugham had never lost links with Paris forged during his earliest years. As a medical student he found the time to slip across the Channel – it could be done at such little cost in those days – to revisit the scenes of his childhood. He was highly aware of the writings of Flaubert and Zola, and of the dispassionate, descriptive exactness on which they insisted. Maugham became a disciple of their most brilliant disciple, Guy de Maupassant, whose stories and novels he devoured, sometimes reading them standing at the bookstalls when he could not afford to buy the books. Maugham admired the Frenchman's precise unaffected prose and the sure hand with which he kept the reader's curiosity constantly alive; he also found his pessimistic view of human nature congenial. It seems altogether appropriate that Maugham's first book should have been written out in three cahiers purchased from the Papeterie F. Brocchi, 30 Faubourg Saint-Honoré, Paris.

A few years earlier a novel had appeared called *A Child of the Jago* by Arthur Morrison, whose *Tales of Mean Streets* (stories appearing originally in *The Strand Magazine*) had marked the arrival of a new genre of fiction based upon the life of the London poor that had been developed in the 1880s by George Gissing. The Jago was the fictional name given by the author to a notorious area of the East End of London, the Old Nichol, a blackspot of crime and violence, eventually demolished and reconstructed thanks to the publicity resulting from the book. The hero of the story is a boy of honest nature who through growing up in such an environment becomes trapped into a life of crime. Maugham, as he admitted later, took Morrison's work as his main model in his study of the slum-life of South London, but he grafted on to it a romantic love-affair which was something of an innovation for working-class fiction at that time. Like Morrison, Maugham aimed to show his heroine's chance of escaping into a decent life doomed by the fact that she belongs to Vere Street, Lambeth.

A Lambeth scene, recalling the Bank Holiday outing in Maugham's first novel.

LIZA
OF LAMBETH

BY

William Somerset Maugham

LONDON
T. FISHER UNWIN
Paternoster Square
1897

Fisher Unwin was impressed by the book but his regular reader had his doubts in view of the sordid life depicted in it. Luckily the publisher then gave it for a second opinion to that great discerner of talent Edward Garnett, who, in an overwhelmingly favourable reaction, was quick to spot the chief influence. 'Mr Maugham,' he wrote, 'has not produced so forceful a study as *The Jago* – but when all is said and done *A Lambeth Idyll* is a very clever realistic study of factory girls and coster life ...' His recommendation was 'Publish' – which was what Fisher Unwin agreed to do. Maugham, who was then working hard for his final examination in surgery, was summoned to his office, and in a state of great elation signed an agreement. After a delay to allow the London literary world and the Press to recover from Queen Victoria's Diamond Jubilee, the novel was published in September 1897, but not as part of The Pseudonym Library. The triumph of the story, the heroine, was underlined by its final title, *Liza of Lambeth*, and it appeared under its twenty-three-year-old author's own name, William Somerset Maugham, in order that he should receive both the plaudits (if any) and the brickbats in his own person.

In the event there were plenty of both, amidst the large number of reviews the book attracted in newspapers and periodicals. *The Academy* was withering about the influence of Morrison which it described as 'deliberate and unashamed mimicry', summing up the work as a 'sordid story of vulgar seduction.' *The Athenaeum* found the portrait of life in Lambeth done with 'uncompromising fidelity and care'; *The Bookman* thought the author was 'very clever ... But he has nothing new to tell' ... It was 'all very hopeless, and unrelieved by any sense of strong feelings in the writer. And yet he is clever, and should be heard of again – in other scenes, let us hope.'

The ripples set in motion by the book even spread to the pulpit of Westminster Abbey where Basil Wilberforce, a great advocate of temperance and later Archdeacon, made it the subject of one of his Sunday night sermons to the delight of Maugham's landlady. Across the Channel in *Le Journal des Débats* Augustin Filon wrote about Liza at the end of October, in an article on '*Le peuple de Londres et le roman naturaliste*' in which he sadly pointed out one failure of realism, '*Liza se perd a dix-huit ans; c'est quatre ans plus tard que la moyenne.*' (Liza was ruined at eighteen, four years later than average.)

Shortly after *Liza* appeared Maugham passed his final examina-

'During the time I was at St Thomas's Hospital I went systematically through English, French, Italian and Latin literature.' The library at St Thomas's

tions and the Senior Obstetric Physician offered him a minor appointment. If there was any doubt in Maugham's mind it was settled by the fact that a second edition of the novel was called for within a month of publication. All that he had dreamed, planned, worked for so industriously, seemed as if it was being turned into reality. He turned down the offer and set about releasing himself from the shackles of medicine. Another kind of release came at the same time: the month that saw the fulfilment of his ambition to publish a book saw the granting of the deepest, darkest desire of his boyhood, the death of Henry Macdonald Maugham in his seventieth year. Both Willie and his older brother Harry, who was also trying to be a writer, went down to Whitstable to attend the funeral of the Vicar. Maugham was now free to turn his uncle into one of the most enduring and grimly comic figures of English fiction.

Maugham was always bursting with ideas for a new story or a play as soon as he had completed the current one. Fisher Unwin urged him to continue in the genre of slum fiction for his next book but Maugham rejected this advice and decided to try something completely different. In his last period at the hospital he had taken time off to visit the Reading Room of the British Museum where he had made a study of the Italian Renaissance. It was there in Macchiavelli's *History of Florence* he found the bones of the plot for his next book. He turned his imagination away from the labourers and seamstresses of South London towards an extravagant world of dukes and despots, popes and poets, courtiers and *condottieri*, with their raven-haired, olive-skinned mistresses.

In this project Maugham had been influenced by some words of the Scottish man of letters, Andrew Lang, who said that a young author should concentrate upon historical fiction because he lacked sufficient experience for anything else. Maugham very soon came to regard this piece of advice as the most arrant nonsense, and it was only towards the very end of his creative life that he turned again to writing historical novels, but now in his early twenties he followed Lang's dictum with enthusiasm. He spent his last summer vacation in Italy learning to read Dante in the original and visiting the places he wished to use as a setting. Before long he had finished his novel which took the form of a memoir by an ageing monk, a blood-spattered tale of seige, intrigue and assassination.

Among the parts of Italy visited by Maugham at this time which did not feature in the novel was the Island of Capri. It was beginning to be the haven of English and Americans who wanted to pursue a private dream. Maugham shared a villa with E.F. Benson, one of the three distinguished sons of an Archbishop of Canterbury. One would give a lot for some detailed records of their conversations, which ought to have contained some fairly sparkling talk of which Wilde himself might have been proud. All we do know for certain is that the young Maugham was still troubled by the ultimate questions that had first begun to exercise him at Heidelberg. One afternoon he scrambled up the rocks behind the villa to observe the blue sea against the blue sky with the distant hazy outline of Vesuvius and he cried out: 'I can't understand it. I don't know, I don't know.'

Someone else who had retreated to Capri as the nearest refuge on this earth to an ivory tower was Maugham's old friend John Ellingham Brooks whom he now despised for his dilettante way of life. Brooks was still declaiming the quatrains of Omar, which he was

The painter Romaine (née Goddard) another member of Bohemian society in Capri, who married John Ellingham Brooks.

trying to set to music, and also translating the sonnets of the French symbolist poet, Hérédia. A curious fate lay in store for Brooks in the shape of an American heiress called Romaine Goddard who was to arrive on the island a year or so hence to pursue her vocation as a painter while discovering her own lesbian nature. She married Brooks, from whom she separated after a few weeks. He sponged off her for the rest of his long, unproductive life. The story of that curious non-marriage is told in Meryle Secrest's effervescent biography of Romaine, *Between Me and Life*.

Morally speaking Capri in the 1890s was rather like England or the United States today: any kind of sexual relationship was not only permissible but socially acceptable. At twenty-two Maugham was no longer an *ingénu*, he had learnt the facts of life as a student in London. Now on Capri, he must have become gradually aware of his own sexual nature and needs. The white spaces between the entries, the self-censored parts of *A Writer's Notebook* speak volumes during these early years.

Several inhabitants of the island would have felt a keen sense of shock at a set of events that had recently occurred in London: the public humiliation of Oscar Wilde at the Old Bailey in 1895. With his own theatrical ambitions seething in his brain, Maugham, must have watched in horror. Wilde's name was removed from the posters advertising his plays; the career of the brilliantly successful society playwright ground horribly to a halt; the darling of the aesthetes was brought low. The trauma of the trial of Wilde goes some way to explain the wary silence of writers whose first books were published around the turn of the century, such as Maugham and E.M. Forster, on the subject of homosexual love.

Not that Maugham had at this stage ruled out the idea of a relationship with a woman. I have heard several friends of Maugham say with a smile that the original of Milly in *Of Human Bondage* was probably a waiter but I maintain until someone produces positive evidence to the contrary that she was a woman as in the book (and as in the earlier version of the book as we shall see in a moment). And when Maugham speaks of a sloe-eyed Spanish girl Rosarito – 'It was not love I felt for you, Rosarito: I wish it had been; but now far away, in the rain, I fancy (oh no, not that I am at last in love,) but that I am just faintly enamoured – of your recollection' – at least we must give him some marks for trying.

Maugham encountered Rosarito, if she really existed, in Seville whither he had gone after the publication of *Liza*. From his youth onwards his outlook was cosmopolitan, and after he had finally left the hospital for good he spent the best part of a year travelling, sight-seeing and working in Spain. His childhood Vicarage browsings in *The Thousand and One Nights* had led him to Lane-Poole's *The Moors in Spain* which led him to Ronda, to Cordova, to Granada, to an exploration of Andalucia on foot and on horseback. An avid linguist, he learnt to speak and read Spanish with the same facility as he had learned Italian the year before, and gained his knowledge of Don Quixote and Don Juan from the originals. He visited cathedrals, mosques and monasteries; he went to carnivals and to bull-fights, to cafés and music-halls where he listened to songs 'like a barbaric necklace in which all manner of different stones are strung upon a single cord, without thought for their mutual congruity'. This trip marked the start of Maugham's lifelong addiction to Spanish culture.

Maugham spent some considerable time in Seville where he wrote short stories and another novel. This time the subject was a slice of contemporary life as experienced by a sensitive young man clearly based on Willie Maugham. It was called *The Artistic Temperament of Stephen Carey*. The manuscript of it is at present in the Library of Congress to whom Maugham donated it in company with that of the book written some twenty years later which superseded it, *Of Human Bondage*, on the understanding that it should never be published. Permission to read it is granted to the student of Maugham's works.

The story begins like that of its successor with the death of the hero's mother; then it describes his years at Tercanbury School but these are not dwelt upon at length nor does he have a club-foot. He leaves school at sixteen, goes to Rouen not Heidelberg, has an affair with his niece's governess (as in *Bondage*) after which most of the remainder of the book tells of his love-affair with a waitress in a London teashop whose name is given as Rosie Cameron. This is the heart of the matter. The sexual wounds by whomsoever they were inflicted were still open, still sore.

On his return to London, Maugham went to see his publisher and he was shattered to learn from that formidable gentleman that his total earnings from *Liza* were twenty pounds. He discovered that in writing there is often a world of difference between *réclame* and reward. However Fisher Unwin was preparing to publish *The Making of a Saint* in May 1898, and he was given *The Artistic Tem-*

perament of Stephen Carey to consider publishing after that. Maugham took a flat near Victoria Station which he shared with Walter Payne, a friend he had met originally in Heidelberg who was now working as an accountant; he stocked it with writing materials and he filled notebooks with reams of dialogue for plays as well as turning out more fiction. He had become a professional writer and he was determined to make a success of that treacherous and difficult calling.

'I can only wish that I had remained a doctor for three or four years instead of writing books which have long been dead as mutton,' wrote the mature Maugham reviewing this obscure period. However at the time his life would appear to have been far from disagreeable. Unlike many aspiring writers he always had enough money for the necessities, even for quite a few of the luxuries. Walter Payne seems to have been the ideal flat-mate – a nice reliable undemanding sort of chap, who went punctually to his office every morning, leaving the place to Maugham, who was thus able to establish that routine of four hours writing in complete solitude that he kept up for the rest of his life. In the evenings Payne would frequently bring young women home, and when he had finished with them he would pass them over to Maugham: a sordid but seemingly satisfactory arrangement.

Whatever sexual adventures he had, none was allowed to interrupt the steady flow of words. He succeeded in placing some of his stories in periodicals, a magazine called *Cosmopolis* (with contributions in English, French and German) published one with a Spanish setting, 'Don Sebastian' in 1898, his first ever to appear, and *Punch* accepted a couple more after that. He soon had enough stories for a book which he called *Orientations*: Fisher Unwin published it in 1899, two years after *A Making of a Saint* which had not only received some encouraging reviews but which had been bought by an American publisher, L.C. Page and Company of Boston. Where Fisher Unwin jibbed, though, was at *The Artistic Temperament of Stephen Carey*, or rather he jibbed at the £100 advance that Maugham with the hubris of youth demanded for the work. The author then tried it on several other publishers, none of whom wanted it at any price. Naturally he was hurt by the barrage of rejection but grateful later for having been saved from publishing an inferior book instead of the eventual *magnum opus*.

Maugham's social life extended well beyond the flat. His growing reputation as an author brought him invitations from hostesses who cultivated literary young men. Later on in novels he would satirize such gatherings mercilessly but at the time he quite enjoyed them. One may picture the short, dapper young man with his somewhat ascetic face, neatly parted hair and gimlet eyes, tossing off his tart observations in a stuttering voice that evoked the spirit of Wilde and *The Yellow Book*. Incidentally, *The Yellow Book* lasted until April 1897, thus almost over-lapping with *Liza*. It did not end with Oscar's trial. The book that Wilde was holding when he was arrested was in fact a yellow-jacketed novel by Pierre Louÿs but everyone thought it was the notorious literary miscellany whose offices were stoned the next day. It turned grey over-night, as 'Dodo' Benson put it – its last numbers contained work of social realism as well as dandified elegance.

Both these moods would be under discussion at the literary gatherings Maugham attended through people like Mrs Wilberforce, the wife of the Archdeacon of Westminster, and traces of both are still to be found in the work he produced at this time. If he did not really belong as a writer to the world of Max Beerbohm, he did not belong to that of H.G. Wells either. The eclectic flavour of his youthful taste may be savoured in an anthology he edited. Known as *The Venture* it was edited jointly by Maugham and Laurence Houseman and appeared in 1903 and 1905. It followed *The Yellow Book* formula of a mixture of stories, poems, essays and illustrations. Although it only survived for two numbers it had a wide spectrum of contributors from Violet Hunt (Ford Madox Ford's mistress whose parties Maugham attended) to James Joyce and is notable for the appearance of Maugham's first published play, a one-act piece *Marriages are Made in Heaven*.

Among the hostesses whose houses Maugham visited during these London years of endeavour and experiment the lady he recalled with the greatest affection was a Mrs George Steevens, one of those people who serve the arts by bringing others together. When Maugham knew her she was an old woman with beady eyes who wore fantastic hats. What made her especially admirable to him was her chequered past and the courage with which she had survived it. As a result of her involvement in the divorce of Dilke she had been banished from society many years before and then she had married George Steevens of *The Daily Mail* who was killed at Ladysmith. Now in her widowhood she lived in Merton Abbey where Nelson's mistress Emma Hamilton had once held court.

Mrs Steevens, who had the outspoken candour which Maugham

FIRST

OPPOSITE
Sir Henry Arthur Jones, the playwright,
who first predicted a career as a
dramatist for Maugham.

always admired, enjoyed the company of writers, actors, painters
and bohemians. Max Beerbohm was sometimes to be seen at her
luncheon parties during the years from 1898 onwards when he was
dramatic critic of *The Saturday Review* in succession to Bernard
Shaw, and so was one of the leading playwrights of the period,
Henry Arthur Jones. Like Beerbohm he became an acquaintance
of Maugham's and when he read *Liza* he said shrewdly that the
story revealed a great dramatic sense. Jones had four daughters.
Maugham remembered one occasion after the youngest of them,
Doris, had made a runaway marriage to William Thorne, a lawyer,
when she was only sixteen. The newly-weds were brought to Merton
by the dramatist to see Mrs Steevens. Henry Arthur Jones fulmi-
nated to Maugham about the marriage. 'I do not think,' Maugham
commented, 'he took the young things' rashness as seriously as
he pretended. The indignation he showed was a tribute he paid to
his sense of decorum, and he was half-humourously conscious that
he was play-acting for a little while he assumed the role of the
outraged Victorian parent.'

Maugham became of friend of Doris Thorne's but it was her
sister, Ethelwyn Sylvia (always known as Sue), three years older
than she, who was destined to play a crucial role in his life. She
was a voluptuous creature, likened by Maugham to Rubens' portraits
of Helen Fourment, and in 1902 she married Montague Vivian
Leveaux. This marriage however was dissolved. Some time around
1904 she appears to have met Maugham at Mrs Steevens's house
when she had become an actress of sorts and had the reputation
of being highly promiscuous with her favours. It was his first
encounter with the woman who was to provide him with his most
famous female character, Rosie in *Cakes and Ale*.

Although the temptation is strong to rush ahead in pursuit of
Rosie, let us go back for a moment to Maugham's literary work in
the last years of Victoria's reign. He was writing plays assiduously
but he was going to have to wait until 1903 before he had a chance
to see one of them performed. To market his fiction he acquired
a literary agent, William Maurice Colles of the Authors' Society,
historically the first of his kind. Maugham followed the collection
of short stories, *Orientations*, by *The Hero* in 1901, a novel about
an officer whose faith has been shattered by his experience of death
in the Boer War, and who returns home to a complacent English
country village. For this book Maugham had parted company with
Fisher Unwin and had gone to Hutchinson where they had

arranged for the anti-evil-eye to be stamped on the binding. Unfortunately they put it upside down. He never allowed this book to be reprinted. (However, he did use the plot again in one of the plays he wrote in the 1930s, *The Unknown*.)

As he laboured at his writing in his London flat Maugham pined for Southern Italy and for Capri. By chance a book had just appeared which intensified this longing. It was George Gissing's autobiographical work of travel in Southern Italy, *By The Ionian Sea*. Maugham wrote a review of the book in *The Sunday Sun* for 11 August 1901. So far as I know it was the only time in his life that Maugham ever wrote a book review. In it he praised Gissing for emulating the French and like Loti blending his own emotions with his observations. Altogether Maugham finds the book charming; he warms to its spirit of escapism into a classical past, and he adds his own footnotes to Gissing's laments for the changes wrought by road and railway developments upon the familiar landmarks of the old Italy. Above all, he admires the vivid simplicity of Gissing's style, its avoidance of Pateresque purple patches, its effectiveness in depicting the hard life of the Italian peasant. Indeed it is not so much a review he is writing – Maugham always declared he had no talent for journalism – as an affirmation of fellow-feeling with the author of the book. Maugham tells us that,

I took it with me to the Kentish coast, and read it in the evenings within sight and hearing of the grey sea, my limbs happily tired after the day's golf. And it was a strange contrast to turn my mind, filled with the brilliant colour of Calabria to this Northern Ocean, cheerless and cold even in mid-July; the sky was like a vault of slate, hanging very low, and at the horizon joining insensibly with the broad flat stretch of sea. It is good to read sometimes books which are so entirely restful, just as after the turmoil of London, with its unceasing roar, which seems to thunder away even through one's sleep, it is comforting to come to the barren, marshy coast of North Kent, peaceful in its unbroken monotony; it is good after the more vivid mental exercise which the manifold interests of the day force upon one, to seek repose in such quiet and leisurely reading. It freshens one to travel easily with Mr Gissing to those exquisite places with their memories and regrets. And if at first the recollection of the scenes and people I love with all my heart made me wretched because I must remain yet another year away from them, I comforted myself with the thought that after all it is in reminiscenses that people and places have their greatest charm.

Maugham used this leaden Kentish backcloth as a setting for his own next book, the novel *Mrs Craddock* (1902), which in its plotting of the path by which the heroine's marriage to a local farmer crumbles gradually into disaster, showed impressively the author's power to construct a longish story with great singleness of purpose. *The Merry-Go-Round* which came next, in 1904, was deliberately diverse: linked episodes about a number of different characters in a variety of melodramatic situations (one provided the plot of his play *A Man of Honour*). Some people saw in the middle-aged spinster with her unconventional morality, who is the human pivot around whom the other principals whirl, a resemblance to the author's favourite aunt, Julia Maugham. (Like Miss Ley she gained her independence late in life on coming into her inheritance.)

Colles sold the book to the house of William Heinemann – destined to be Maugham's lifelong British publisher – who insisted upon certain changes in the text. It did not sell well, however. Maugham put the blame upon Colles whom he dismissed, replacing him in due course by the redoubtable J.B. Pinker, who had acted for both Wells and Gissing up to the latter's death in 1903. Maugham was stirred by the example of the book he had reviewed by Gissing to attempt something similar to it himself and the result was *The Land of the Blessed Virgin* (1905), based on material he had gathered while in Andalucia. Although he later suppressed this book in favour of a more mature one about Spain and Spanish culture, *Don Fernando* (1935), it does possess much the same quiet, observant, understated enthusiasm as Gissing's, and it shows Maugham already starting to burgeon into the fine travel-writer and essayist he much later became when his journeys embraced half the world.

At this period of his life when he was a young man of promise Maugham was still in touch with his brothers. Freddie had married in 1896 and although a coolness had already developed between them Maugham was fond of Freddie's wife to whom he sent all his books. Charles, another lawyer who was sometimes known as 'the saint of the family', had joined the firm in Paris, and had married a woman painter known as Beldy. Willie stayed with them when he was in France occasionally. The remaining brother Harry, who had begun life as a lawyer, had switched to literature, but without Willie's genius for it.

It was galling for Harry, who had been trying his hand at poetic dramas on subjects like St Francis, to hear that Willie was about to have one of his plays performed. True, it was not by a commercial management, only by the Stage Society, an organization giving

'Freddie' Maugham at Cambridge in 1889. He afterwards became Lord Chancellor.

neglected plays of merit their chance with a Sunday evening performance and a further matinée. The play of Maugham's they chose
was *A Man of Honour*. One of the selection committee responsible
for getting it on was the journalist W.L. Courtney, a champion of
Ibsen and now editor of *The Fortnightly*. He published the text of
the play as a special supplement to the magazine. It was especially
gratifying to Maugham to have won acceptance among people of
such taste and judgement. The first performance of the play which
tells of yet another disastrous marriage, between a brilliant young
lawyer and a barmaid he has made pregnant, given at the Imperial
Theatre on 23 February 1903, was a great moment in Maugham's
life. It went well and the subsequent notices were encouraging.

The only sour note came at the party afterwards when Harry
turned up late, shabbily dressed, and said in a loud voice: 'I'm glad
to hear that my little brother has had a success at last!' The sad,
envious fellow did not have much longer to live. One day of the
following year Maugham called at his flat in Cadogan Street, Chel-
sea, to discover that his brother had swallowed a dose of corrosive
acid. He lingered for three days in St Thomas's, where Willie took
him, and then he died. Perhaps it was just as well because if he
envied Willie with such bitterness for what he had achieved up to
then what would his state of mind have become later?

But what was Maugham's own view of himself at this time? Not
a rosy one at all as far as work was concerned. Even though *A Man
of Honour* was revived in a commercial production for a few weeks,
his early one-act play was performed in a café theatre in Berlin in
German translation, and he had more plays and novels up his sleeve
with agents and publishers buzzing around him, Maugham was far
from regarding himself as a success. By the age of nearly thirty he
had become highly discontented with his London existence and was
planning one of those uprootings he felt to be vitally necessary from
time to time. Charles had taken a villa at Meudon for the summer,
and while Maugham was visiting him there he met in the garden
an outspoken young man with ginger hair some five years his junior
who was an Irishman, an old Etonian and a painter. His name was
Gerald Kelly. Maugham took to him unreservedly. Kelly had a
studio in Paris and had already begun to make his name. Maugham
wrote to him soon after that first meeting to say that he was moving
to Paris himself and asking him if he could find him somewhere
to live.

4

Golden Sovereigns

Maugham's friendship with Gerald Kelly lasted for the rest of his life. It was based upon an attraction of similarities. They were both small men physically, abounding in energy and power of work. Both had been brought up by clergymen – Kelly's father was Vicar of Camberwell – and both had been educated at an ancient public school. Both of them therefore had had the advantages and training of an English gentleman, and both tried to live as artists. This was a moral conflict which Maugham was to work at in more than one of his novels.

Both Maugham and Kelly were independent of the class from which they gained their start in life but they never completely repudiated it. They relied on its members to purchase their wares, and shared many of its assumptions. They were both outspoken and cosmopolitan, sweeping aside the prevailing idols, Maugham repudiating the aestheticism of Walter Pater, and Kelly making him aware of the Impressionists, but this iconoclasm never crashed the breakwaters into revolution. They both lived through revolutionary periods in the arts during which the whole basis of the arts they practised was radically altered; they both watched the revolution from the grandstand, as it were, but neither ever seems to have felt the urge to enter the arena himself and take up the banner.

The ambience of the artistic revolution, as it enveloped the working painter and the young hopeful, steals from chapters in *Of Human Bondage* which Maugham based upon his year in Paris in 1905. 'I entered a world new to me of men devoted to the arts,' he said in *Looking Back*. Unlike Philip Carey he was not actually studying to be a painter himself, he was trying to write genteel society comedies which would win him fame and fortune in the theatre. But he was in and out of Kelly's studio in Montparnasse, much of the time living within walking distance in an apartment near Lion de Belfort, at 3 rue Victor Considérant. Kelly's activities in Paris while

One of the earliest of Gerald Kelly's portraits of Maugham. This one was painted in 1907.

Maugham was there are chronicled with admirable detail by Derek Hudson in his biography, *For Love of Painting* (1975). Kelly knew people like Paul Léautaud, the diarist, and Marcel Schowb, the writer who nourished a dream to go to the South Seas and meet Robert Louis Stevenson but who was prevented from ever accomplishing it by the ill-health which killed him at an early age. Schowb was in touch with the latest developments in the theatre through his wife, the actress Marguerite Moréno. He was also a friend of another English writer who was living in Paris, Arnold Bennett, now in his late thirties and with most of his work still ahead of him. Maugham met Bennett for the first time in Paris. He called upon him for tea, one congenital stammerer entertaining another.

He [Bennett wrote] has a very calm almost lethargic demeanour. He took two cups of tea with pleasure and absolutely refused a third; one knew instantly from his tone that nothing would induce him to take a third. He ate biscuits and gaufrettes very quickly, almost greedily, one after the other without a pause, and then suddenly stopped. He smoked two cigarettes furiously, in less time than I smoked one, and solidly declined a third. I liked him ...

Whether Maugham ever really liked Bennett is more doubtful. He certainly admired *The Old Wives Tale* when it appeared in 1908 but he always regarded Bennett with somewhat amused contempt. He could never quite forgive him for being an upstart and for being blatant about success where Maugham himself was quietly urbane. 'He was cocksure and bumptious, and he was rather common,' Maugham summed it up, adding hastily: 'I don't say this depreciatingly but as I might say that someone was short and fat.'

However they saw each other fairly regularly in Paris because they both used to dine at the same restaurant in the rue d'Odessa, Le Chat Blanc. It was the haunt of a great many expatriate artists and writers who were given a dining-room to themselves by the proprietor where they would indulge in vehemently exhibitionistic arguments as they ate at the tables arranged in a horseshoe-shape. The topic most frequently under discussion was how to represent reality, either by words or with paint. One Englishman who tried out his views there was Clive Bell in the days before Bloomsbury, but he never remembered seeing Maugham. Ivor Back who became a well-known surgeon was another. They were a lively bunch even if some of their names do not mean very much now; people like Penrhyn Stanilaws, the illustrator, Paul Bartlett, the sculptor, Alexander Harrison, the painter, the Canadian artist James Wilson Morrice

ABOVE
Aleister Crowley, 'The Great Beast',
who was British head of the Oriental
Templars. He provided Maugham with
the model for the hero of *The Magician*.

OPPOSITE
Arnold Bennett, whom Maugham first
met in Paris in 1904.

and the Irishman Roderick O'Conor. The two latter, both in their
different ways, made a deep impression on Maugham and provided,
respectively, the models for Cronshaw and Clutton in *Of Human
Bondage*, as did Gerald Kelly for Lawson and Stanilaws for Flanagan.

Maugham learnt about the problems involved in representing the
quality of light and the distortion of the human form in the interests
of greater realism. He discovered that those famous horizontal
nudes, the *Odalisque* of Ingres and the *Olympia* of Monet, heralded
a new era, that the art of painting had moved a long way since
the days of Raphael and Leonardo. O'Conor was a minor Impres-
sionist who had already exhibited work in the Salon. He had small
private means and lived in Paris permanently. He also possessed
a wide-ranging knowledge of literature and laid down the law across
the soup with a ruthless and pugnacious sarcasm. His dogmatic
authority affected Maugham who pricked up his ears when he heard
O'Conor speak about the times he lived and worked at Pont-Aven
in Brittany with a stockbroker turned painter called Gauguin.

In *Of Human Bondage* we get a taste of the ideas and attitudes
current in the cafés of Montparnasse at this time, but the place
where we must go to find a complete description of a dinner at Le
Chat Blanc is a much less well-known novel of Maugham's, of which
afterwards he was rather ashamed, called *The Magician* (1908). It
was inspired by a flamboyant and manic figure whom Kelly had
known at Cambridge and who burst upon the restaurant while
Maugham was there and who soon would carry off Kelly's sister
as his bride. This was Aleister Crowley, drawing-room mystic, self-
styled satanist and scatological poet. He stayed for a time with Kelly
in his studio. Maugham's intense dislike of Crowley did not prevent
him taking a professional interest in him. I think we may fairly
conjecture that in some way the over-bearing charlatan wounded
Maugham verbally at the dining-table and Maugham's habitual
response to a verbal wounding was to write a book. In the event
it was not a very good book apart from those early pages in the restaurant, and Crowley had the last laugh when he reviewed it in
Vanity Fair ('The author bless my soul! No other than my old and
valued friend, William Somerset Maugham, my nice young doctor
whom I remembered so well from the dear old days of the *Chat
Blanc*. So he had really written a book – who would have believed
it!') but the novel is also interesting to the biographer of Maugham
for the admiration it shows for the will-power of the magician which
transcends his charlatanism.

As Arnold Bennett showed just now in that revealing glimpse, this was the overwhelming impression made by Maugham at this time – the strength of his will. He seems to have been prepared to go on writing plays until the cows came home in order to get one put on. His agent, Golding Bright, had good contacts in the theatre in both London and New York and from time to time reported tantalizing nibbles. One American impresario, George C. Tyler, was after the play with which Maugham at last achieved a production, went to see him in Paris and was impressed by the fight he was putting up for recognition.

Maugham aimed to keep his name perpetually before the public if not as a playwright then at least as a writer of books. Sometimes he would rapidly turn a rejected play into a novel to bring in some ready money, as he did with his mischievous comedy about an amorous vicar (shades of Parson Maugham?) in *The Bishop's Apron* which appeared as fiction from Chapman and Hall in 1906. When he cannibalized this play and another one in similar fashion he had needed the cash to escort a young person of expensive tastes around the town, but by the time the money came through the affair was over and he used it instead to go on a trip to Egypt.

His year in Paris had been marvellously educative but he was on the move again and had returned to London as his base. While he had been away Walter Payne had moved to an address in Pall Mall where Maugham now took rooms too. In the early chapters of *Cakes and Ale* he has transposed these lodgings to Half Moon Street, the other side of Piccadilly, where the struggling writer scratching a living from literature is surprised to receive an urgent summons to lunch by a fashionable novelist. Like the narrator of that book Maugham at this time was alone and biddable. He was a member of the Bath Club where he and Payne would sometimes play bridge. His main excursions into the world of the intelligentsia were Mrs Steevens's gatherings at Merton Abbey. On one of these occasions Max Beerbohm took him aside suggesting in the nicest possible way that, in spite of the modest success he had had with *A Man of Honour*, the theatre was too crude, too vulgar a place for a talent so fine and delicate as his. Fiction was his true métier and he should stick to it.

Maugham nodded assent and appeared to take the point. However he did not have the slightest intention of abandoning his most cherished ambition. There was, he felt, a part of his talent which could please a wider audience than he had so far reached and he was determined to exploit it. Apart from Beerbohm another member of Mrs Steevens's circle whom Maugham saw again was Sue. One evening in 1906 he took her out to dinner and invited her to come back with him to his rooms in Pall Mall where, he says, he began a love-affair that was to last on and off for eight years.

During its off periods he continued to travel on the continent with Spain and Southern Italy acting as the more powerful magnets. Some of these trips were financed by the sale of stories to magazines. In the first decade of the century Maugham contributed fiction to *The Strand Magazine*, *The Sketch*, the *Daily Mail*, *Bystander*, *Illustrated London News*, *The Lady's Realm* and *Pall Mall Magazine*. In 1908 he had sold a story for twenty pounds, which would be equivalent to two hundred today, and he was exploring the classical ruins of Sicily waiting for the cheque to arrive. His funds were dangerously low. Maugham was in Girgenti when the news came through for which he had been waiting half a lifetime. He heard from Golding Bright that a comedy he had written called *Lady Frederick* was about to go into production. Even such a master of self-control as Maugham might have let out an exclamation of joy at the information. At any rate his passion for Greek temples was for the moment abated and he put his mind to the problem of how he could return to London in time for the first rehearsal.

What had happened was that the manager of the Court Theatre in Sloane Square, one Otho Stuart, had had an unexpected flop and he needed to follow it with something in a hurry. The play he wanted to do next was not immediately available and Goldie had, like the good agent he was, brought *Lady Frederick* to his attention. The Court, then as now, was a minority playhouse and Maugham's comedy was not really the serious sort of drama that Stuart wanted to put on there. However he was desperate and he thought it might fill the hiatus for six weeks, so he decided to go ahead with it.

Maugham arrived in Naples with five shillings in his pocket and not much more than that in the bank, the cheque having not yet arrived. He bluffed his way through the shipping office obtaining not only a ticket for Marseilles but also five pounds in cash (golden sovereigns in those days). The luck continued to hold on board when he won the sweepstake on the day's run. He arrived back in London with a shilling left, just enough for a cab. As he entered the Court Theatre in time for the first rehearsal he felt, he said, like Phileas Fogg after his journey round the world in eighty days entering the Reform Club as the clock struck eight.

OPPOSITE
Ethel Irving in the final act of *Lady Frederick* when she forces her young admirer to observe her applying her make-up.

His luck held both throughout the rehearsals and during the first night. Lady Frederick – the character for whom Mrs Steevens had served as a model – was depicted as a ruthless enchantress. By the time the final curtain came down she had succeeded in enchanting not just the ordinary playgoer but those hard-faced gentlemen, the professional dramatic critics. They welcomed a new talent. Maugham's comedy did not just play for six weeks: it ran for the best part of a year.

Just as *Liza* betrayed 'unashamed mimicry' of Arthur Morrison, so the machinations of Lady Frederick reveal how assiduously Maugham had studied the plots and the people and the paradoxes of Wilde, Pinero and his beloved's father, Henry Arthur Jones. Lady Frederick twists everyone around her elegant Irish little finger and then just when you think she is going to move in for the kill she lets everyone off the hook.

Imitative in many respects it may be, but no playwright can succeed with the public by imitation alone. It is already apparent that Maugham had his own way of manipulating an audience, more artfully than Wilde, more cunningly than Pinero or Jones. There is no precedent in their work for the scene that prevented the play from getting on the stage for so long, in which the heroine deliberately disillusions her young lover by summoning him to her boudoir and letting him see her face as it really is in the cruel light of day before she applies the paint and the powder that restores her vanished youth. In our era of *carte blanche* this episode appears to be quaintly amusing: in 1908 it was a sensation.

The success of *Lady Frederick* whetted the public's appetite for more. Maugham and Goldie enjoyed the gratifying sight of managements competing to put on plays which previously they had rejected. A. and S. Gatti secured *Jack Straw*, a comedy about a royal refugee in London, and put it on at the Vaudeville Theatre in March with Charles Hawtrey. The American Charles Frohman (who was to be Maugham's main impresario until his untimely death in 1916 on the *Lusitania*) and Arthur Chudleigh got *Mrs Dot*, another comedy about a seemingly wicked widow, and presented it at the Comedy Theatre in April with Marie Tempest. The actor manager Lewis Waller produced himself in *The Explorer* at the Lyric Theatre in June; the theme was conduct unbecoming during an expedition into darkest Africa. Meanwhile *Lady Frederick* in the form of Ethel Irving swept all before her. She moved from the Court to the

Garrick in March, to the Criterion in April, to the New Theatre in June, and to the Haymarket in August.

Thus in the *annus mirabilis* of 1908 Maugham had four plays running in London at the same time, a record that still remains unbeaten to this day. (Alan Ayckbourn equalled it in the 1970s but only thanks to a trilogy running on different evenings at the same theatre.) Suddenly from being one of a host of hard-working authors trying to earn an honourable living, Maugham had become the most applauded and successful playwright of the day. The accolade from the Press for this feat came when *Punch* printed a cartoon by Bernard Partridge depicting the piqued and pensive figure of Shakespeare standing in the street with his back to the billboards advertising all four Maugham plays. The accompanying editorial comment offered a mock interview with the new wonder:

'At last,' said MR PUNCH, 'I have the pleasure of meeting you. I know your name so well, but this is the first time I have been able to put a face to it.' And he shook England's Dramatist warmly by the hand. 'Let me see,' he went on, 'you have twenty-three plays running in London just now, I think?'

'Twenty-four,' said the Dramatist modestly.

'You must be a man of many parts,' hazarded MR PUNCH.

'Well, of course I –'

'There are one or two things about which I should like to talk to you. I have seen your name so often on programmes, hoardings, and – if you will forgive me for mentioning it – motor-omnibuses, that I feel I know you quite well.'

'You are very kind,' said England's Dramatist.

'A playwright,' continued the Sage, 'particularly a twenty-fourth playwright, must have a great knowledge of affairs. Also by long practice, he must have achieved the art of projecting himself into the personality of others. Tell me then, what do you think of the new fashion in women's dress?'

'Woman,' said the Dramatist, 'is cutting off her petticoats to increase her hats.'

'Pardon me,' said MR PUNCH gently, 'but I was not for the moment addressing MR SOMERSET MAUGHAM, the brilliant epigrammatist, but one of his many heroines. I wish for an expert opinion.'

'Then I may tell you in confidence that there is very little in it.'

And so on . . . The epigram under the submerged influence of Wilde was still in fashion when Maugham began writing plays and he dutifully included several. However, it did not really suit his comic manner and he welcomed its demise. In fact, the epigram survived only

in France in the Wildean career and work of Jean Cocteau. In England dialogue was becoming closer and closer to the tone of ordinary speech. An actor like Hawtrey brought the understated speech of the English gentleman on the boards to perfection. Noël Coward used to say that he had learnt all he knew about acting from Hawtrey. Maugham, who learned much about the technique of comedy from him too, was fascinated by the art with which he concealed his art. 'No one,' said Maugham, introducing Hawtrey's memoirs, 'could say a line with the naturalness of Charles Hawtrey, so that when you heard him you said, "he speaks exactly as though he were in a drawing-room, it is not acting at all"; and yet it was acting all the time, art and not nature, the result of his instinctive sense for the stage and his experience; and the line was said not as it would have been said in a drawing-room but as it needed to be said in order to get over the footlights.' The whole of Maugham's own technique of playwriting is implicit in that observation. He emerged as the supreme exponent of a new form of naturalism.

But what effect did his success have on him personally? He answered that question in his *Notebook*: 'Success. I don't believe it has had any effect on me. For one thing I always expected it, and when it came I accepted it as so natural that I didn't see anything to make a fuss about. Its only net value to me is that it has freed me from financial uncertainties that were never quite absent from my thoughts. I hated poverty. I hated having to scrape and save to make both ends meet. I don't think I'm so conceited as I was a year ago.' But perhaps he was not quite so unmoved by his triumph as he claims.

If one were to try to argue the critical case for Maugham as a playwright one would not lean too heavily on these early pieces which do not revive particularly well today. Certainly he dismissed them as apprentice work. However, they do show a shift of emphasis in the concerns of drawing-room comedy towards the overwhelming importance of money in the social balance of power. Maugham's realism penetrates the crust of the convention he inherited from Henry Arthur Jones. He – or she – who pays the piper calls the tune. This was a perception, obvious if you like but hitherto somewhat blurred through preoccupation with social standing and adulterous lapses, a perception to which society however reticent on the subject itself responded instantly. It was a theme for social comedy which in Maugham's hands was to prove well-nigh inexhaustible in the years to come.

The plays' success meant that from now on money was something that Maugham would never lack – his income quadrupled at once. Now when he went to stay in country houses he could hand the butler a tip commensurate with that received from the other male guests. He was soon besieged by invitations and he began to move in circles of political power and influence. Like many young authors who suddenly leap into prominence he began actually to meet on equal terms the company he had been writing about. He would stay with people like the Allhusens at their place in Stoke Poges where the other guests formed 'a pleasant medley of lords, politicians, society beauties, soldiers, sailors and authors'. Among the young politicians to be met there was Winston Churchill and his wife the American beauty, Clementine Hozier. Maugham played golf with Churchill on the nearby links and began a friendship that was to last for the remainder of their lives. Among the men of letters Edmund Gosse, the critic, who also held the post of Librarian at the House of Lords, 'was', said Maugham, 'the most interesting and consistently amusing talker I ever knew'.

On the whole, though, he was not greatly impressed by the conversation at such gatherings, and he was highly amused by the arrogant assumption of the politicians that the British Empire was a pocket borough whose highest offices were in their private gift. Maugham expressed his astonishment at this attitude in the first few pages of *The Summing-Up*, and he used his observations to even more devastating effect in his great comedy *The Circle* (1929) which, set in the country house of a rising politician, contains a famous scene where the old roué says that had he become Prime Minister he would certainly have given his mistress India.

Maugham's ascent of the social ladder may be plotted topographically by the houses he occupied in these London years. As we have seen he began in Victoria, then moved to Westminster and on to Pall Mall. Now as a successful playwright, he moved to lodgings in Mount Street, near Berkeley Square, and finally after a couple of years, as the money continued to flow in he purchased the long lease of a house in Chesterfield Street in the heart of Mayfair. He called it pointedly 'the house that Frohman built' as he invited his impresario and benefactor to be the first dinner guest on one of his frequent visits to London. He was elected a member of the Garrick Club. Walter Payne, who had also prospered in more conventional areas and become a director of several companies, lived in Chesterfield Street and kept a friendly eye on Maugham's

Charles Frohman, 'angel' for Maugham's early plays. He was drowned in the *Lusitania* disaster in 1915.

OPPOSITE
Maugham established himself as a
playwright well before the First World
War: here Marie Tempest (with
Graham Browne) stars in his
Edwardian comedy *Mrs Dot*.

ever-ramifying financial affairs; but gradually the playwright was
moving altogether out of his sphere. Success mellows people, as
Maugham often said, but it also erodes certain friendships.

One night as Maugham walked home from the Comedy Theatre
where *Mrs Dot* was playing he observed that Panton Street was
bathed in the glow of a beautiful Turneresque sunset. He thought to
himself 'Thank heaven I don't have to try to find words to describe
it.' At the age of thirty-four, after a decade of work as a professional
writer, he had come to the conclusion that the hardest part of the
job lay in visual description. Dialogue flowed from his pen with a
ready facility and he had no difficulty in contriving dramatic situations in which to extend his characters, but the task of describing
their appearance and their location was painful. He heaved an immense sigh of relief at the thought of liberation from the effort of
visual writing. From now on, apart from a few brief descriptive sen-
tences at the start of an act to indicate the setting, that side of things
could be safely left to his producers and designers.

However, he still had a couple of novels soon to appear. His Paris
story 'The Magician' appeared in 1908, and so did the novel
from which he had drawn the least successful of his plays *The
Explorer*, with a hero based upon H.M. Stanley. But by the time
they were published Maugham was indifferent to the reception of
these books, and he was glad to get out of further contracts for fiction
which his agent had been in the process of arranging for him. He
wrote now two more sparkling light comedies, *Penelope* and *Smith*,
'to consolidate my hold upon the public', both of which were produced in 1909. Four years later came that memorable piece, sparked
off by Frohman's suggestion he should write an up-to-date version
of *The Taming of The Shrew*, *The Land of Promise*. It was based
on a trip he made to Canada to stay with some relatives and it shows
what happens to a genteel English spinster when she gets to Manitoba. Frohman, who was promoting Maugham in America, pre-
miered the play in New Haven in 1913 with Billie Burke and it
opened on Broadway before London. There were also plays produced which he quarried from his early fiction like *The Tenth Man*,
Grace and *Loaves and Fishes*, plays full of strong situations but
which have not stood the test of time; and – to round off his dramatic
output up to the start of the First World War – there were two trans-
lations from the French, Grenet-Dancourt's *The Noble Spaniard*
and Molière's *Le Bourgeois Gentilhomme* which in a hideously cut
version was performed as *The Perfect Gentleman* by Sir Herbert

Beerbohm Tree in 1913 as a curtain-raiser to Strauss's *Ariadne in Naxos*, not one of Maugham's happier ventures.

But on the whole, as the runs enjoyed by several of the above proved, he did have a most happy and seemingly effortless knack of knowing how to please the public. He tried altering his sights from the bankrupt aristocracy to the prospering middle-class. *Smith* gave a taste of satirical things to come. The title refers to a parlour-maid whose mistress spends her copious leisure afternoons playing bridge with a ghastly crew of acquaintances. During one of these sessions the news comes through that the baby of one of the women is sickening: eventually we hear the news of its death but the players continue with their game regardless. The hostess's brother is so appalled that he marries Smith, the only decent human being among them. 'Bridge or babies?' asked *The Times* in its review while arguing that this choice was too starkly exclusive to be true, that the playing of the former did not necessarily prevent the successful rearing of the latter.

It was a perfectly valid objection; none the less the unjust equation produced some effective scenes. Maugham's contempt for most of his characters was withering, people like the young man who is a kind of afternoon lap-dog for Smith's mistress. Even uglier was the scorn of the bridge players for the concern shown for the dying child by its father who is Jewish. The *pièce noire* element in the whole picture surpassed in its blackness anything to be found in Maugham's predecessors in the English drama of the domestic interior. The raven-like shadow of Henry Becque hangs over it. A.B. Walkely in *The Times* recognized the Gallic kinship in Maugham's plays and so did J.T. Grein in *The Sunday Times* who objected in this one to 'the repeated references to the Jews in terms of ungraciousness'. He thought that in the scene of the baby's death, 'Mr Maugham drives cynicism to the highest pitch'. Thus around this time we begin to hear much about a creation of the critical pen, Maugham the Cynic. Over the years it was a label which stuck.

5

Jester into Spy

Maugham the Cynic was most exquisitely seen in the portrait painted in 1911 by Gerald Kelly called *The Jester*. It is as if he were some Symphony in Brown and Gold. No dandy of the 1890s gazed upon the beholder with greater disdain than the seated Maugham pictured here in his immaculate formal dress, his tall top-hat and lightly clasped cane. It was painted partly as a joke, just as the fictional portrait of Maugham by Oscar Wilde's friend Ada Leverson ('The Sphinx') in her novel, *The Limit*, published in this same year, was a joke. Here we are told that the much courted playwright 'Hereford Vaughan', honoured guest at every dinner party, was 'not even embittered by success'.

But was that really so? Behind his public mask Maugham was suffering agonies. Success had brought deprivations as well as rewards. True, he had had his revenge upon the parsimony of his childhood in the vicarage as well as on his family for frowning upon his ungentlemanly choice of career, but his reputation among his literary peers had suffered a sea-change. In his innocence Maugham had demanded from the Bitch-Goddess not only fame and money but also respect. He found that like some evil wizard in his boyhood reading she gave him only the bitter barmecide feast of notoriety.

Among the many interviews with him in the first flush of his emergence as a playwright there was one in which he said it was no business of drama to concern itself with ideas. This unguarded observation brought down coals of critical fire upon his head. His friend Max Beerbohm, who had been forced to eat his words, albeit urbanely, about drama not being Maugham's métier, turned on him in the pages of *The Saturday Review* before retiring for good from dramatic criticism. Maugham had had Shaw in mind and his Nietzschean arias: all he meant, all he ever meant, was that theatre should aim to entertain. His own plays had succeeded handsomely

OPPOSITE
Max Beerbohm by Charles Condor.
The young Max was the theatre critic
of *The Saturday Review* when
Maugham's first plays were produced.

in doing precisely that by the traditional method of strong construction and teasing the audience's curiosity. Somehow, though,
by reaching a wider audience than the members of the Stage Society
he had forfeited his right to be considered a serious author. Out-
wardly he shrugged it off; inwardly it pained him and continued
to do so for the rest of his life. But quite apart from this wounding
sense of critical rejection, Maugham soon discovered within himself
the seeds of dissatisfaction with the prose drama. He had plenty
of plays he wanted to write but he became more and more conscious
of how inherently ephemeral a form it was. He resented the imputation that his comedies were merely flippant frothy trifles; on the
other hand he did reluctantly agree that the prose play did not offer
a writer the opportunity for going into his characters in depth as was
possible in the more private experience of the novel. There was one
character particularly whom Maugham wished to explore closely
at this time – himself. He may have proved his virility as a money-
earner (and indeed in other ways) but the wounds inflicted upon
him during his early years in London when he had suffered pro-
longed sexual humiliation had in a curious way been reopened by
his years of triumph in the theatre, or perhaps his triumph made
him aware that they had never really healed.

Thus his apparent release from the toil of fiction-writing proved
to be illusory. In order to purge himself of the past, Maugham reckoned he would have to write a very long novel. A rough blueprint
for it existed already in the rejected manuscript, *The Artistic Temperament of Stephen Carey*, but he needed now to go more deeply
into the causes of his peculiar sense of alienation from life in the
midst of so much prosperity, to follow his own emotional and intellectual progress throughout those early years with great but not
absolute fidelity to fact. Could he present himself objectively?
Could his training as a novelist steeped in French naturalism be
applied to such a project? Could he re-structure his life into a series
of episodes, into a story that would hold the attention of the reader
from beginning to end? 'Madame Bovary – c'est-'moi', said Flaubert
identifying with the frustrations of his heroine. From Liza of Lambeth and Mrs Craddock of Kent to Penelope of Harley Street,
Maugham had identified successfully with the frustrations of different types of modern women, now he felt an overwhelming
impulse to identify with his own frustrations as he so vividly recalled
them.

But he needed a huge empty space of consecutive time to work

all this out. It was impossible to combine the labour of such a project with the pressures of the theatre. He therefore decided to close down the play-factory for a year, perhaps two. Frohman was horrified at the prospect of his most money-spinning author shutting up shop in this fashion and for such a long period. If Maugham's aim had been merely to make a lot of money out of his writing, as his detractors claimed, then his decision was unthinkable. In those days there were few extended runs and no movie and TV rights; however much in demand your plays were you needed to keep at it consistently, as professionals like Pinero and Henry Arthur Jones had proved. For someone so financially astute, the decision to stop just when he had got going was either crazy or it was the gesture of a serious, self-confident artist.

At any rate once he had made up his mind he was not the man to be deflected from his aim. He withdrew from the stage and from society and set to work. He concentrated upon the figure of his club-foot hero Philip Carey with his thin skin, his pride, his inexperience and his massive power of assimilation. For two years Maugham lived backwards. What others pour out indiscriminately into the ear of an analyst, Maugham shaped and polished with the joy of a craftsman. No doubt there were precedents for such a novel of quasi-autobiography in the work of the Victorian novelists, but no one hitherto had sailed quite so close to the winds of real events and real people. Maugham's detachment from himself when young, his depth of understanding of his own character, introduces a new dimension into this type of novel. It is a work in which he excels not merely as a genre-painter giving us a series of insights into life at the close of the Victorian period but also as an exponent of the art of self-portraiture.

While Maugham was thus obtaining his catharsis from the emotional woundings and rejections of the past, a further rejection by a woman lay in store for him. His affair with Sue Arthur Jones continued intermittently while he lived at Chesterfield Street. She had obtained her divorce from her first husband and was succeeding in getting some small parts as an actress and understudy work. Although they never mentioned the matter Maugham felt that she wanted him to marry her. As the prospect of his fortieth birthday dawned upon him Maugham seems to have felt the need to be married. He certainly cannot have been in any doubt about his homosexuality but in spite, or more probably because of it, he wanted the social conformity, the respectability in appearance of marriage. He made up his mind he would marry Sue. He knew that she had been to bed with most of his friends and he was not in love with her but she had a sweet smile and he was truly fond of her. She was appearing in a play in the United States at the same time as Maugham's affairs demanded that he visit America where he now had a considerable reputation as a dramatic author.

Maugham crossed the Atlantic and before he left England he tempted Providence by purchasing a wedding-ring. He met Sue when she arrived later at New York harbour and as she came down the gangplank he noticed her chatting gaily to a dashing young man. Maugham and Sue met and kissed but they only had time for an hour or so together before she had to go with the rest of her company to Chicago. Maugham followed her there three weeks later when his business in New York was concluded and booked a suite in Sue's hotel. He invited her for supper after the show and made his proposal. He suggested they should marry straight away, go to San Francisco and then from there to Tahiti, somewhere he had been planning to visit for a long time in order to do the research for a novel about Gauguin which he had been brooding over ever since he had heard about the painter from O'Conor.

To Maugham's total incredulity she turned him down flat. He thought at first she must be just stalling, but no, she meant it. She did not want to marry him. However, she was perfectly prepared to go to bed with him. Maugham put the ring back in his pocket and left. That was the end of Sue so far as he was concerned. It was also the beginning of Rosie in *Cakes and Ale*. Back in London a few weeks later where he succeeded in trading back the ring for the original purchase price less ten per cent, Maugham noticed a placard for the *Evening Standard* which said, 'ACTRESS MARRIES EARL'S SON.' A vision of the dashing young man on the gangplank came into his mind. He was Angus McDonnell who became the second husband of Sue in 1913.

Towards the end of that year Maugham was sitting in the Chesterfield Street house reading when the phone rang. It was a Mrs Carstairs who lived in the next house but one and was the wife of the London representative of Knoedler, the picture dealers. Someone she had asked to a theatre party had dropped out at the last minute and would he like to come along? Apart from the Carstairs the other guest was a Mrs Wellcome, an attractive, well-groomed, striking woman in her middle thirties who was separated from her husband – the founder of the drug-manufacturing firm of Burroughs Well-

88

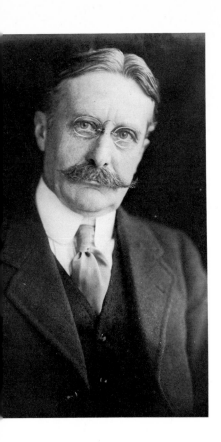

come. She was known to her friends as Syrie. This lady who was
to play a highly controversial part in Maugham's life had had a
singular history. Her grandfather was a Jewish refugee called Barnado who had fled from German anti-semitism in the 1840s to
Dublin where he had become a Christian convert and married. His
son Thomas, the famous Dr Barnado who founded the homes for
destitute children, was Syrie's father. She was brought up in England where as a young girl she met Henry Wellcome who was interested in her father's work and whom she married at the age of
twenty-two when he was forty-eight. The marriage lasted only
about five years and when she met Maugham she had been separated
from him for a decade. She led a life of fashion and elegance
in London. One of her most devoted admirers was another London-
based American, H. Gordon Selfridge who had started his Oxford
Street Department Store four years earlier while in his early fifties
after many years as an employee of Marshall Field in Chicago.

Despite the devotion of this leonine character, who had a flair
for public relations way ahead of his time and a passion for attending
theatrical first nights, the friendship between Maugham and Syrie
ripened. They saw each other frequently throughout the remainder
of the year. In February 1914 Maugham had a first night of his
own coming up, that of the London production of *The Land of
Promise* at the Duke of York's Theatre with Irene Vanbrugh as the
heroine. He gave Syrie tickets for it and afterwards he attended a
house-warming party she was holding. It was thus an evening of
double triumph after which they were constant companions. In the
Spring they went to Paris together and then to Biarritz from where
they drove to Spain in Syrie's car. As the fateful summer of 1914
began to unfold their paths temporarily diverged. Syrie went to
Rome and Maugham to the villa on Capri where he invited Gerald
Kelly to stay. When the Great War started they decided to stay on
for a while.

Syrie joined them on the island and then somewhat reluctantly
they all made their way back to England. Soon after his return
Maugham contacted Winston Churchill who was now First Sea
Lord to see if he could find him a job but the best he could offer
at that time was clerical work at the Admiralty. Maugham wondered
if his fluency in French could not be put to good use. He heard
that the Red Cross were sending a fleet of ambulances to France.
He applied to join the unit as an interpreter. Before long he was
in khaki and on his way across the Channel.

Scenes from *The Land of Promise*, 1914, Maugham's treatment of the *Taming of the Shrew* theme. The action is set in a log cabin in Manitoba.

The unit was dispatched to Northern France and eventually to Poperinghe in Flanders. Maugham was within 25 kilometers of the fighting. He saw plenty of the action during this early period of the war in the form of wounded from both sides who flooded into the makeshift hospitals where he worked. One young German soldier had to have his leg amputated and in his distress he imagined that he was being operated upon in this way because he was one of the enemy. Maugham had the task of explaining to him that it was the only means of saving his life. As a qualified doctor Maugham also found himself put back to the basic job of swabbing and dressing wounds, but in all his years at St Thomas's he had never seen anything of this order. 'There are,' he wrote, 'great wounds of the shoulder, the bone all shattered, running with pus, stinking; there are gaping wounds in the back; there are wounds where a bullet has passed through the lungs; there are shattered feet so that you wonder if the limb can possibly be saved.'

They were constantly on the move and at each billet Maugham's *Notebook* would come out. He went to the Cloth Hall at Ypres where he was nearly killed as a shell hit it. He discovered a nobleman's library at Montdidier; he observed the English colony at Amiens; he chatted with a Flemish landlord with a gnomic manner at Steenvoorde. His companions in the Unit were a mixed batch of English and Americans of various rank. One of them, Desmond MacCarthy, had already begun to make his name as a perceptive judge of books and plays. He and Maugham briefly shared a billet. It was the start of the respect in which the two men held each other throughout their careers. MacCarthy wrote several substantial essays on Maugham at various times. In one he recalls how during this harrowing period the galley proofs of *Of Human Bondage* arrived. Maugham laid them out in strips on the bed correcting them by the light of a guttering candle. He made extremely few marks on them. When MacCarthy commented upon this Maugham explained that he always went through his work very carefully before sending it to the printer.

Another member of the Unit was a young, handsome American called Gerald Haxton. He was one of those people it is splendid to be with at a time of physical danger – resourceful, courageous, gay, companionable, and with nerves of steel. Maugham found him immensely attractive and under the stress of war an instant friendship was formed. In many ways it was a friendship of opposites in that their temperaments were as different as that of the ant and

ABOVE
An ambulance unit in the early days of
the First World War.

OPPOSITE
The young Churchill, pictured in
Westminster in 1915, a life-long friend
of Somerset Maugham.

the grasshopper. Where Maugham was self-contained, private, secretive almost, conserving everything for his work, Haxton was outgoing, extravagant and, as the years were to show, an incurable alcoholic. When the work of the Unit came to an end and its members scattered Maugham and Haxton planned to meet again. Gerald went back to the States with the vague idea of finding a job and Maugham to Rome where he was joined by Syrie and where he proposed to write a play. As a contrast to the horrors of the Front, the theatres of the West End of London were enjoying an unprecedented boom as havens of escape for men on leave. Maugham saw no reason why in the intervals between his war service he should not continue his career as a playwright.

His liaison with Syrie had given him insight into a world of which hitherto he had been perforce innocent: it was a world where people spent money like water. To enter it you needed to possess either vast wealth or some kind of ancient title, preferably both. It was the current version of the international set. It had its base in England but had been penetrated by Americans, particularly well-endowed

American women who had acquired the titles and style of ancient but impoverished European ducal families. In the luxurious drawing-room and the well-appointed country house of such a woman, Maugham saw matter for a peculiarly gamey and fragrant comedy of manners which he called *Our Betters*. He had been struck especially by what Syrie had told him of her relation with Gordon Selfridge and he introduced the character of a doting man of trade complaisantly paying the bill for the extravagancies of his near nymphomaniac mistress. Maugham dipped his pen in gall as he wrote, finding great energy in his disgust.

He also turned his mind to more practical ways of helping with the war. Here again Syrie provided him with inspiration. She had a friend who was the mistress of someone high up in Intelligence. She arranged a meeting between this gentleman and Maugham as a result of which it was proposed that he should go to Switzerland, a hotbed of espionage. While living there, behind his front of play-writing, Maugham would be able to work as an agent for the Department. With his perfectly genuine 'cover' and his fluency in different languages, Maugham appeared to be ideally qualified as an operator.

Of Human Bondage appeared on 12 August 1915, the American edition from George H. Doran Company preceding the English from William Heinemann by one day. The original dust-wrapper with a surprisingly mature Philip Carey in a wide-brimmed black hat and a cape had to be suppressed because it showed the club-foot as the right and not the left. It was a substantial book for a young Tommy to pack up in his old kit bag to take to read while in transit and not one likely to cause him to smile, boys, smile, all that often. He would have been better off with Conrad's *Victory* or Buchan's *The Thirty-Nine Steps* or even perhaps D.H. Lawrence's *The Rainbow* among the other English novels that appeared in this same year. Its Darwinian gloom undoubtedly contributed to the neglect of Maugham's book when it first came out. The professional book-reviewers, who were still functioning in spite of the hostilities, were bothered and baffled by the book. They complained that the hero was unlikable, that it was not one novel but several and that the image of the pattern in the Persian carpet with which the author sums up his moral position was an evasion. In the *New Statesman* Gerald Gould shillied and shallied, while *The Athenaeum* anonymously animadverted that, 'In such long novels reiteration is peculiarly tiresome and apt to reduce the gratitude which should be felt for the detailed portraiture and varied aspects of life the author presents to us.' So much for two years' hard labour. It was left to a fellow-novelist in the realistic tradition, and an American, Theodore Dreiser, to give the novel the authoritative and affirmative review it so desperately needed. His article 'As a Realist Sees It' published in the *New Republic* on Christmas Day 1915, turned the tide once and for all by recognizing the novel's seriousness and importance.

Maugham himself in his new role as a secret agent was fortunately remote from all this activity of the critical mind. He was having to adjust to yet another new profession, one that he found highly stimulating and to which, with his flair for assessing other people's weaknesses, he was admirably suited. His first assignment was in Lucerne to investigate an Englishman who was living there with his German wife. Afterwards he put this little mission to good use in a story 'The Traitor' which appears in *Ashenden*, a volume based upon his wartime service in Intelligence. (Apparently there were fourteen further stories relating to this period which were never published and the manuscripts of which he burnt for fear of infringing the Official Secrets Act.) His headquarters in Switzerland were in Geneva where he established himself in a hotel bedroom ostensibly writing plays (which he was also actually doing) while making contact with other Allied agents of various nationalities and making a weekly journey into France on the steamer across Lake Leman to Thonon. His passport was not stamped when he arrived on French soil and as the steamer went from Switzerland to Switzerland there was nothing when he arrived back in Geneva to suggest that he had not been to Vevey or Lausanne. However Maugham always felt a chill of apprehension as he returned to base lest the Swiss police had discovered what he was up to, and would pop him into gaol for the duration.

In another Ashenden story, 'Miss King', Maugham finds two hefty cops waiting for him in his hotel bedroom; it is some time before he discovers that they have come merely to make a routine inquiry about noise from the casino. Maugham projects himself as the sardonic bachelor man of letters, enjoying his strange new role with humorous resignation, finding neat analogies between the pitfalls facing a spy and a book-reviewer. But in reality while he was in Geneva this monastic dedication to his mission was interrupted by the presence of Syrie. She too had good reason to be out of London where her divorce at long last from Henry Wellcome was competing for headlines in the gutter press with the war news. Maugham found it difficult to entertain her in the midst of his other concerns and the fraught world of espionage, with the various agents playing complex games of double-bluff with each other in the hotel lounges and bars, was not one in which her own social gifts had much chance to flourish. She became very bored and after a few weeks returned to England.

Eventually a sense of boredom began to afflict Maugham too, and with the material for several stories to be written after the war was over lodged in his *Notebook*, he applied to his chief to be released. His gusty, rain-sodden trips across the lake had affected his health and he now had a touch of tuberculosis, the disease that had killed both his mother and his aunt. His discharge was granted and he returned to London. He resumed relations with Syrie and the question of marriage arose.

It so happened that he had been dealing with two mature lovers who suddenly find themselves free to marry, and are somewhat shattered by the prospect, in the comedy he had just written, *Caroline or The Unattainable*. Like the man in the play Maugham wished to postpone the event for the moment. One reason was that Syrie's divorce had not yet been made absolute; another was that he was determined now to go to Tahiti to investigate the life of Gauguin for the novel which he had been turning over in his mind for so long. A final reason was that he wished to see Gerald Haxton again.

He therefore made his way to New York and contacted Gerald, who was in Chicago and at a loose end. When Maugham proposed that Gerald should accompany him on his trip to the South Seas the offer was accepted with alacrity. Their reunion was marred slightly by the appearance in New York of Syrie who not unnaturally was reluctant to let Maugham go off without her. However he was very firm with her. He explained that it was a working journey, that he would not be gone for more than three or four months, that by the time he got back her divorce decree would be absolute and they could marry. Unwillingly Syrie complied. So Maugham and Gerald set off together.

OPPOSITE
Gerald Haxton, Maugham's companion on his travels and later his secretary.

6

Eden and After

Maugham was not the first English writer to go on a pilgrimage to the South Seas. Robert Louis Stevenson had spent his last years on Samoa where he died in 1894. More recently in 1913 and 1914 Rupert Brooke had wandered around the islands for several months, visiting Stevenson's grave at Vailima, and staying in some of the regions soon to be explored by Maugham and Gerald. Brooke knew all about the painter who was the object of Maugham's quest. 'You may figure me,' he wrote to Eddie Marsh, 'in the centre of a Gauguin picture, nakedly riding a squat horse into white surf.' The mood of such a voyage was caught by Brooke in another letter to Marsh: 'Romance. That's half my time. The rest is Life – Life, Eddie, is what you get in the bars of the hotels in 'Frisco, or Honolulu, or Suva, or Apia, and in the smoking rooms on those steamers. It is incredibly like a Kipling story, and all the people are very self-consciously Kiplingesque. Yesterday, for instance, I sat in the Chief Engineer's cabin with the First Officer and a successful beach-comber lawyer from the white man's town in Samoa, drinking Australian champagne from breakfast to lunch. Today I am not well.'

Kipling never actually wrote any stories about the white settlers in the South Seas and their relations with the native population. The writer who was to make that contribution to the literature of colonial experience was in 1916 on his way from San Francisco to Honolulu. Like Brooke he sat on the seaside verandah on the Moana Hotel in Honolulu taking drinks as the sun went down, eavesdropping (as all writers do) on the conversations around him, scooping up Life in rich, gleaming hauls, to be salted away in the *Notebook*.

There is a myth current among people who write or tell knowing stories about Maugham, one he encouraged, that he was so self-conscious about his stammer when in the presence of strangers that he shut up like a clam, leaving all the talking to Gerald. It was – so the myth goes – Gerald who sat up all night getting drunk with the planters and beach-combers. Gerald would then totter back to his cabin and wake up the sleeping Maugham with some wonderful bit of gossip he had just heard while his companion in his pyjamas got out his *Notebook* and wrote it all down, to be turned later into 'The Letter' or 'The Out-Station'. There might be some tiny grain of truth in this somewhere, but it is rather misleading. Certainly wherever they went Gerald would spend a considerable amount of time in the bar. He was, as they say, a Hail-Fellow-Well-Met. Certainly, too, Maugham was a reserved individual, not given either to getting drunk every night, nor to slapping people on the back heartily and calling them 'Old Man'. He was also a powerful wit, a challenging arguer and, when he wanted to, capable of charming the birds off the trees. I am prepared to believe that he drew great strength from his association with Gerald whose company he enormously enjoyed when Gerald was not behaving impossibly (which was quite a lot of the time) and relied on him a great deal in practical matters like getting the car to start. I am much less convinced that he found him indispensable in eliciting material for fiction out of white men in their cups.

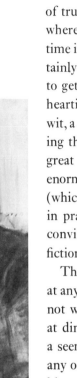

The truth is that Maugham could find a good story anywhere at any time. His flair did not mysteriously vanish when Gerald was not with him. He could sense a story in someone he sat opposite at dinner before he or she had hardly opened his mouth. It was a seemingly effortless knack he possessed to a greater extent than any other modern English writer. Often the stories seemed to seek him out, to land ready-made in his lap in their finished form. A striking instance of this concerns the genesis of the most famous story he ever wrote, the one which originally appeared as 'Miss Thompson', and afterwards came to be known as 'Rain'. The material for this story came to Maugham in November 1916 when he and Gerald left Honolulu to go to Apia.

On board the steamer were three people among his fellow-passengers who particularly caught Maugham's attention: an American couple, the husband being a medical missionary, and a single lady. Maugham documented the whole voyage carefully and made detailed notes about these three people. The missionary had 'a cadaverous look, and a look of suppressed fire'. His wife 'was a little woman with hair very elaborately done, with prominent blue eyes behind gold-rimmed *pince-nez*; her face was long like a sheep's, but she gave no impression of foolishness, rather of extreme alertness ... She spoke of the depravity of the natives in a voice nothing could

Nuuana Avenue, Honolulu – a typical
residential thoroughfare photographed
in the early twentieth century.

OPPOSITE
Jan Eagles as Sadie Thompson in the
play that was made from Maugham's
famous story 'Rain'.

hush ... described their marriage customs as obscene beyond description.' The single lady is summed up thus: 'Plump, pretty in
a coarse fashion, perhaps not more than twenty-seven: she wore
a white dress and a long white hat, and long white boots from which
her calves, in white cotton stockings, bulged. She had left Iwelei
after the raid and was on her way to Apia, where she hoped to get
a job in the bar of a hotel.'

Because of a quarantine inspection the passengers found their
journey delayed. They were forced to stay for a time in a scruffy
two-storey lodging-house near the dock in close proximity to each
other. Maugham also described their temporary abode: 'The owner
is a half-caste with a native wife surrounded by little brown children.
The rooms are almost bare of furniture, a poor iron bed with a
ragged mosquito curtain, a rickety chair and a washstand. The rain
rattles down on the corrugated iron roof. No meals are provided.'

All the main elements of 'Rain' are here, *données* offered to the
grateful author by life itself. Far from it being a question of clumsy
Life at her work again, as Henry James used to scorn reality for
bruising the precious particle, Life here appears to be the senior
partner in the collaboration, leaving Maugham little more to do than
to act as a competent newspaper reporter. One American writer
about Maugham, Wilmon Menard in his *The Two Worlds of Somerset Maugham*, has even managed to discover the passenger list for
this voyage and to note on it the name, together with those of
Maugham and E.G. Haxton, of a Miss Thompson. Maugham did
not trouble to change it.

It all seems so easy, but of course it isn't really. Anyone can
wander into Rouen Cathedral at any time and gaze up at the stained-
glass window in the north aisle which depicts the life of St Julian
in some thirty scenes, but you need to be Flaubert to write 'La
Légende de Saint Julien L'Hospitalier'. The same process of rigorous selection and editing and alteration, of bringing the given
elements into dramatic confrontation and resolution, goes on in
Maugham's apparent transcripts from reality as it does in
Flaubert's. The words of the fiction-writer produce an alchemical
illusion in the mind of the reader, the illusion known as realism.

In Apia they met the administrator of the island and after a few
moments' conversation Maugham was guessing that though he ran
his island competently he was excessively insistent on insignificant
details and had the standards of the public schoolboy. It was,
according to Menard, another island administrator, Dick Williams

ABOVE
Gauguin: stockbroker to painter.

OPPOSITE
Tahiti at the time Maugham was there:
Rue de la Petite Pologue, Papeete.

on Savaii, the largest island of Western Samoa, who was the model
for Maugham's most tyrannical white ruler, the brutal Mackintosh.
And yet another whose alcoholism inspired 'Before the Party'.
Maugham and Gerald explored Savaii, Apolima and then went
back to Apia to go to Suva in Fiji and from there to New Zealand.

During these journeyings Maugham observed the last era of
colonial society, its paternalism, its rigid division between the rulers
and the ruled, its attempt to impose Western institutions and values
upon the local inhabitants. He met a wide spectrum of humanity
including not just the officials of the British government, but mis-
sionaries eager for souls, traders greedy for copra, chieftains and
their tribesmen. He visited the English clubs and the local brothels.
He noted how many of his countrymen spent half their lives pickled
in alcohol. Like Rupert Brooke before him he was astonished at
how closely the English people resembled characters out of
Kipling. 'There were men,' said Maugham, 'scattered about the
outlying parts of the Empire who would never have been just what
they were except for him.'

The works of Gauguin had led him to expect land- and sea-
scapes of paradisal loveliness and in this too he was not disappointed.
One of the most magical came when, on the second leg of their tour,
they approached Tahiti with Murea its sister island in view. A gaily
coloured crowd had gathered on the quay at Papeete to greet the
steamer, the women conspicuous in their bright floral garments.
Maugham soon detected a mixture of foreign influences upon the
place which 'as a whole, notwithstanding its English and American
stores, its Chinese shops, has a subtly French character'. By 1916
Gauguin had already been dead for twelve years but the scent was
still warm and it was not long before Maugham had begun to ask
the vastly obese and agreeable Madame Lovaina of the Hotel Tiare,
(so named after the white star-shaped bloom which is the national
flower of the island) about the painter. The trail led the two
men about thirty-five miles out of Papeete to the house of the widow
of a chief who had been awarded the *Légion d'Honneur* when the
French occupied the island. She told them, as she sat on the floor
in her shabby black Mother Hubbard, puffing away at a native
cigarette, that there were pictures by Gauguin in a house nearby, and
called for a boy to show them the way. Maugham and Gerald took
him with them in their car. After a couples of miles' journey which
ended in a swampy grass path they came to a dilapidated frame
house. Here is how Maugham described what they found there:

The master of the house, a flat-nosed, smiling dark native came and talked to us. He asked us to go in, and the first thing I saw was the Gauguin painting on the door. It appears that Gauguin was ill for some time in that house and was looked after by the parents of the present owner, then a boy of ten. He was pleased with the way they treated him and when he grew better desired to leave some recollection of himself. In one of the two rooms of which the bungalow consisted there were three doors, the upper part of which was of glass divided into panels, and on each of them he had painted a picture. The children had picked away two of them; on one hardly anything was left but a faint head in one corner, while on the other could still be seen the traces of a woman's torso thrown backwards in an attitude of passionate grace. The third was in tolerable preservation, but it was plain that in a few years it would be in the same state as the other two. The man took no interest in the pictures as such, but merely as the remembrances of the dead guest, and when I pointed out to him that he could still keep the other two he was not unwilling to sell the third. 'But,' he said, 'I shall have to buy a new door.' 'How much will it cost?' I asked. 'A hundred francs.' 'All right,' I said, 'I'll give you two hundred.'

I thought I had better take the picture before he changed his mind, so we got the tools from the car in which I had come, unscrewed the hinges and carried the door away. When we arrived back at the chiefess's we sawed off the lower part of it in order to make it more portable, and so took it back to Papeete.

The unscrewing and sawing was performed by Gerald rather than by Maugham. Eventually the Gauguin painting on glass (Gauguin's young mistress seen as Eve in the Garden of Eden) found its way into Maugham's writing-room in the Villa Mauresque.

The trip to Tahiti led not merely to Maugham acquiring this tangible evidence of Gauguin's genius, it also yielded a rich crop of seedlings for his fiction. Out of it came two of his finest books, *The Moon and Sixpence* (1919), in which he turned Gauguin into an Englishman, and *The Trembling of a Leaf* (1921), sub-titled 'Little Stories of the South Sea Islands', containing 'The Pacific', 'Mackintosh', 'The Fall of Edward Barnard', 'Red', 'The Pool', 'Honolulu' and 'Rain'. These were the first stories Maugham published after his youthful efforts, and they revealed his immediate mastery of the form. Apart from these books the South Sea experience remained as a bank of inspiration upon which he was always able to draw, and we find it still playing a part in a comparatively late work like *The Razor's Edge*. Nor should one forget the forty-five pages of the *Notebook* under the year 1916 (from which I have quoted above) which provide such a readable factual record of the trip.

If Gauguin had gone to Tahiti to release himself from the toils of marriage and to concentrate on his art, Maugham returned to America to find the prospect of marriage looming before him inescapably in the person of Syrie who was now a free agent. He said goodbye to Gerald who went back to Chicago to try to find employment. It seems that shortly afterwards Maugham married Syrie before a Judge in New Jersey. He was forty-two and she was thirty-seven, and soon she was to present him with a daughter. What his motives were it is impossible to say with any certainty beyond that they were complex and not susceptible to glib instant analysis. One of them undoubtedly sprang, paradoxical as it may seem, from his vocation as a writer. He believed in trying everything, and marriage was the one universal experience which he had not yet had.

A Tahitian Eve painted on a glass-panelled door by Gauguin and transported to the South of France by Maugham.

Maugham and Syrie Wellcome shortly
after their marriage.

Before long the newly-weds were back in New York where they
had plenty of friends and acquaintances. One member of the English
community there was a relative of Maugham's. He was a plump,
boyish-looking Englishman in his early thirties – a baronet, a Wyke-
hamist and a Cambridge boxing blue. In peace-time he had been
a merchant banker, then Captain in the Duke of Cornwall's Light
Infantry and had fought in Flanders in 1915 where he had been gassed.
Now he was to all intents and purposes in charge of the American
and Transport Department of the British Ministry of Munitions.
His name was Sir William Wiseman. After he had met Maugham
a few times he had a proposition to put to him.

7

Wiseman's Agent

William Wiseman's real job in the United States was Head of Intelligence Operations. His activities have been the subject of a scholarly study by W.B. Fowler, *British–American Relations 1917–1918: The Career of William Wiseman* (Princeton 1969), who describes him as one of the pioneers of twentieth-century diplomacy. I am indebted to Mr Fowler's book in what follows.

Wiseman had a naval background and had been in Mexico before the war where he became an agent for the firm of Kuhn, Loeb. He gained the confidence of Woodrow Wilson through the special relationship he had with the *eminence grise* of Wilson's foreign policy, Colonel Edward M. House. It was Wiseman and not our Ambassador, Sir Cecil Spring-Rice, who provided the hot-line during the war between the British and United States Government, especially after the fall of Asquith in 1916 when Lloyd George headed the Coalition Government.

One aspect of foreign policy on which both these allies were in agreement was the urgent need to counteract German propaganda in Russia. Their fear was that Russia was about to make a unilateral peace with Germany, particularly if the Provisional Government were to be overthrown by the Bolsheviks. Someone was needed to go to Russia on the delicate mission of keeping her in the war. Wiseman decided that Maugham with his previous experience of intelligence work was admirably suited for the job. He proposed that he should act as an agent in Petrograd and investigate the situation, with the back-up of prominent refugee Czech nationalists under their leader Professor Thomas Masaryk.

Maugham hesitated. It was one thing to keep one's eyes skinned and one's ear to the ground in neutral Switzerland. It was a much taller order to go on a journey of more than a thousand miles in the middle of winter knowing only half a dozen words of Russian to try to prop up the weak and tottering Government. Moreover those

bitterly cold nights crossing Lake Leman in a draughty steamer had taken their toll. Maugham had had a touch of tuberculosis in Switzerland, now he had begun to spit blood. He went to see a New York doctor who told him his lungs had been affected. Maugham then explained the journey he was proposing to undertake and at whose behest. The doctor replied that normally he would have recommended a sojourn in a sanatorium for a month or so, but that as there was a war in progress, Maugham could risk it. Maugham went back to Wiseman and told him he was willing to take on the job.

Maugham also informed Syrie, who raised no objection. He was instructed to consult several prominent Russian Jews in New York, including a Rabbi Wise and members of the American Czech community who were active in the cause of an independent state of Czechoslovakia. After various background briefings of

OPPOSITE
Sasha Kropotkin, a portrait by Gerald
Kelly.

this kind, Maugham sailed for Tokyo on 28 July 1917 with authority
from Wiseman to draw up to $21,000 for the mission. From
Japan he went to Siberia, then by rail to Petrograd. At the same
time a party of four American Czech patriots made their way to
Petrograd quite independently from whom he was to obtain
support. These included a tireless exponent of old-fashioned
espionage, Emanuel Victor Voska, a courageous and cunning operator in the cause of his fatherland.

The Czechs and Maugham pretended to ignore each other on
the Trans-Siberian railway. Maugham's companions were three
American diplomats who were on their way to join the Embassy
in Petrograd. They had heard of him as an author. He explained
that he was going to Russia to write about conditions there for the
Daily Telegraph. When they reached Petrograd they found a highly
precarious situation with the Bolsheviks gaining ground daily. Both
Maugham and the Czechs made their headquarters in the Europa
Hotel. Maugham met Voska and became his liaison with the British.
At the same time he established contact with the future President
of Czechoslovakia, Prof. Thomas Masaryk, who knew Wiseman.
Another guest in the hotel at the time pursuing a campaign of her
own was Mrs Pankhurst.

Maugham made his presence in Petrograd felt at the British
Embassy from where he sent his dispatches to Wiseman in cypher;
the key to this was not known to the Embassy officials. Sir George
Buchanan, the Ambassador, was affronted by this secrecy and David
Bruce, his first secretary, made the fact known to Maugham. How
this *froideur* and the even greater coolness between the British and
the American Ambassadors was made to thaw through the good
offices of Maugham will be familiar to readers of the Ashenden story,
'His Excellency'.

Maugham's language problem was solved by the presence in
Petrograd of Sasha Kropotkin, the daughter of Prince Kropotkin,
author of *Mutual Aid*, whom Maugham had known when they were
living in London. This formidable lady is clearly the model for the
femme fatale in the famous Ashenden story 'Mr Harrington's Wash-
ing', also taken from something that actually happened. An American businessman was in Petrograd negotiating a loan by his company to the Russian Government. He told Maugham of the
excellent terms he had negotiated but Maugham and the others said
he would be lucky if the Government was still in office to pay
when the loan matured. When the shooting started Sasha Kropotkin

reported that she had lost track of this American as they went to recover his laundry. He was later found dead in the street humped over a bundle of clean clothes.

Maugham appears to have had in his youth some kind of brief but unforgettable liaison with Sasha. It had ended, he said, 'without acrimony on either side' and she was useful now in introducing him to various members of the Provisional Government under its Prime Minister A. Kerensky. He reminded Maugham somewhat of his old friend, now dead, Charles Frohman. Like the impresario, the Prime Minister had the trick 'of exciting in others the desire to do things for him'. Even so Maugham was not impressed by this worried character in khaki who went around making interminable speeches, apprehensive of his Bolshevik enemies. Kerensky knew that Lenin was hidden away somewhere in Petrograd, but was unable to arrest him.

The one member of the Provisional Government who did strike

RIGHT
Alexander Kerensky *left*, head of the doomed Provisional Government in Russia in 1917.

OPPOSITE
Boris Savinkov, the former terrorist who became Minister of War.

Maugham as being a person of real strength was the former Minister of War, Savinkov. He was an ex-terrorist who had assassinated the Grand Duke Serge and Trepov, the Chief of Police. Maugham found him quiet, reserved and modest; a fascinating talker in good idiomatic French who told him several memorable stories. He had a great contempt for Kerensky who after a disastrous battle in the summer when the Russian troops had been heavily defeated got into the car with Savinkov and made a trite quotation. 'It was characteristic of this man without education,' he told Maugham, 'he should comfort himself with such a bad poet.'

Maugham kept in close touch with the Czechs. In the evening he would meet Masaryk in a café and confer with him over a cup of chocolate. He could not share his optimism. He found the Allies were not popular in Russia and via Wiseman he urged the Allied Ambassadors to show more sympathy towards the Russian radicals.

Apart from the pressures of his secret assignment within this

extraordinarily explosive political situation, Maugham managed to take time off to penetrate the country and to gain valuable insights into the Russian character. In his own profession of literature it was the great Russian writers who were now names to conjure with in fashionable circles. A new Russian word, 'intelligentsia', had come into vogue to describe such circles. Maugham reckoned wryly that he had belonged to it, until the commercial success of his comedies had caused him to be cast into outer darkness. Maugham had read widely not only Tolstoy, Dostoyevsky, Gorki, Turgenev and Chekhov but also Korolenko, Sologub and Artzibachev, and was interested to gain knowledge of their countrymen and the Russian countryside. His admiration for Chekhov, like himself a renegade doctor, remained for the rest of his life even though he deplored his influence on story construction.

In spite of the revolution the ballet and the theatre still flourished and Maugham visited both while he was in Petrograd. The ballet provoked thoughts reminiscent of his young Pateresque self – 'I saw in the fugitive beauty of a dancer's gesture a symbol of life etc etc' – the theatre did not provoke any thoughts at all because he could not understand a word of what was going on. He picked one evening on a nice big theatre and sat down in it to watch the play. He gathered that the piece was a comedy and that the audience to judge by their laughter found it amusing. By the end of the first act he felt that there was something vaguely familiar about the situation; he had a sense of having been here before. He glanced down at the programme and discovered that the play was his own *Jack Straw* translated from the English of 'Mum'.

Maugham's forebodings about the political situation proved all too accurate. As Kerensky continued to make speeches, food and fuel became scarcer and scarcer, while it seemed as if the Germans might make a dash for Petrograd. Maugham had a meeting with the Prime Minister who gave him a confidential message for Lloyd George. Its point was that he did not believe, as the winter came on, his government could carry on for much longer and he requested assistance. On Wiseman's instructions Maugham returned to London via Norway and Scotland early in November and conveyed this personally to Lloyd George, who found Kerensky's proposal totally unacceptable but told Maugham how much he had enjoyed his plays.

Maugham then went to the lung specialist at St Thomas's who advised immediate treatment in a sanatorium. Before he could go

Maugham was summoned to Downing Street again to appear at a high-level meeting of British and American officials. He found an imposing batch of politicians and diplomats among whom he recognized Rufus Isaacs, then special envoy to the United States, and also Wiseman. Maugham was so nervous that he asked Wiseman to read Kerensky's message for him lest he start to stammer. But in the words of Sir Eric Drummond Kerensky's request was by then 'of only historical interest'. On the night of 7 November the Bolsheviks rose; Kerensky's ministers were arrested, the Winter Palace was sacked, the reins of power were seized by Lenin and Trotsky and they immediately sued with Germany for peace. In the confused aftermath of this shattering takeover there was a plan mooted by Sir Edward Carson that the Allies should support General Kaledin to mobilize his Cossack troops and that Maugham should operate with them from Rumania. Maugham informed the meeting at this point of the state of his health. Rufus Isaacs smiled and said: 'Go to your sanatorium and I hope you'll get well very soon.'

Shortly afterwards Maugham went to a sanatorium at Banchory in Kincardineshire in north-east Scotland and was put to bed for several weeks. Syrie visited him and while undergoing treatment Maugham acquired the material for yet another short story about the effect which long incarceration in such a place has upon the emotional lives of the patients. He responded to the treatment and was free to go to live with Syrie in a house they rented by the sea. While he was in this holiday home he wrote the Gauguin novel he had been planning for so long and called it *The Moon and Sixpence*. Thus his first literary act when he became a married man with a family was to write a book about a man of exceptional artistic gifts who escapes from the shackles of marriage with calculated heartlessness and ferocity.

Maugham returned to the sanatorium for the autumn and winter of 1919. The war had ended but rationing was still in force and the black market flourished. Officers and men fortunate enough not to have been killed in the fighting were on their demobilization suffering the grim realities of Lloyd George's land for heroes. Maugham bought a pair of mittens and sat in his room writing a farcical comedy about these returning heroes. He called it *Home and Beauty* (or in America *Too Many Husbands*). This time it all turned upon their immense reluctance to resume the marital responsibility from which the war had freed them.

A scene from *Home and Beauty* with
Charles Hawtrey *centre* glowering at
Gladys Cooper as the heroine, Victoria.

8

East of Suez

Between the end of the First War in 1918 and 1928 when he purchased the Villa Mauresque at Cap Ferrat, Maugham lived in London married to Syrie. It was an unhappy period for him full of a succession of domestic crises, but it was also the period of some of his finest work. The greater his private anguish, the greater seemed his facility and inventiveness. Maugham began now in his fiction to project himself as the mature ironic man of the world confiding his secret thoughts to the reader while leading him down the garden path of his story. You find this Maugham in *The Moon and Sixpence*, looking fondly back upon his obscure, youthful self, turning to the brash post-war young with their sexual candour and their experimental techniques of writing, confessing that as an author he is now already 'on the shelf', yet proceeding at the same time to prepare for the opening shock of his novel with immense authority and charm. This author-mask of Maugham's serves as the kindly reasonable foil to the heartlessness of Strickland who is another persona of the 'real' Maugham.

The Moon and Sixpence was published in the Spring of 1919. It was his first book to follow *Of Human Bondage* and was treated with respect by the reviewers who praised its technique even if they disliked its hero. One reviewer who particularly disliked Strickland without apparently realizing that he was based on Gauguin was Katherine Mansfield. The year before, she had married John Middleton Murry and was now reviewing books for *The Athenaeum* of which he had become the editor. In the course of her review she asked some pertinent questions about the figure of the supposedly great artist present in the novel. 'If,' she said, 'to be a great artist were to push over everything that comes one's way, topple over a table, lunge out right and left like a drunken man in a café and send the pots flying, then Strickland was a great artist. But great artists are not drunken men; they are men who are divinely sober. They know that the moon cannot be bought for sixpence, and that liberty is only a profound realization of the greatness of the dangers in their midst.'

Undoubtedly the greatest danger in Maugham's midst at this time was, like Strickland's, domestic. He and Syrie returned to the house in Chesterfield Street where Walter Payne had been living while they were away. Maugham's former writing-room became Syrie's bedroom, an act of renunciation on his part that boded ill for the future. Syrie sold her house in Regent's Park after Maugham had declined to live there. With some of the furniture from it she started a shop in Baker Street, the beginning of the career through which she became famous in her own right, as an interior decorator and designer. The shop was an immediate success; eventually she

A 1930s drawing-room designed by Syrie Maugham.

moved to more splendid premises in Duke Street, Mayfair. Syrie imposed her own style and elegance upon her clients. Drawing-rooms entirely done up in white and the use of Chinese furniture and motifs were her two most memorable contributions to the tone of the period. She was in her way as much a disseminator of the distinctive, fragrant mood of the 1920s as Nöel Coward.

Even Maugham had to admit that his wife did possess impeccable visual taste. When his plays reached the dress rehearsal stage Syrie would accompany him to the theatre to look at the clothes and the designs. Her word in these areas was law. Fay Compton, who played the heroine in a play he wrote about the wife of the British Consul in Cairo, *Caesar's Wife*, remembered the care Syrie took over her costume and how exquisite was the result. This play, which was performed at the Royalty Theatre in London in March 1919, with C. Aubrey Smith (already playing elderly men with a strong sense of duty), as the Consul was a rather self-conscious effort by Maugham to combat the cynic label. 'I had often been,' he said, 'reproached for writing only about unpleasant people, and, though I did not think the reproach justified, I was not averse from trying to write a play in which all the characters were estimable.' He had just read Madame de Lafayette's novel, *La Princesse de Clèves*, with its exquisite handling of the theme of virtue versus passion within a marital triangle and the work had inspired him to write a play in which modern people behaved with an equal measure of scrupulousness. The result was somewhat atypical of his plays, one in which the lovers' infatuation occurs against a rising tide of Egyptian nationalism. So far as I know it is the only work he wrote set in Egypt. I have never had the chance to see it performed but I think it could still be moving. In the original production Fay Compton was by all accounts very fine. Maugham himself wrote: 'The gesture with which she held out her arms to her lover after she had sent him away for good and all and he had miserably gone had a grace, tenderness and beauty the like of which I have never before or since seen on the stage.'

It will give some idea of Maugham's creative flow in his middle forties, the prime of life for an imaginative writer, when I say that this play, *Home and Beauty*, *The Moon and Sixpence* and *The Circle* were all written between 1918 and 1919. It is *The Circle*, given first at The Haymarket Theatre in 1921, with Fay Compton as the heroine, that has proved to be the most successful of all the plays he wrote. The most recent revival, which transferred to this same

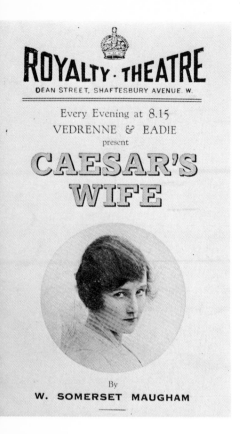

OPPOSITE
Scenes from *Caesar's Wife*, a drama of
virtue.

London theatre in October 1976, does most strongly support
Maugham's view that the piece will serve as his 'baggage for
eternity'. The masterly comic structure has received all the praise
it needs over the years. Let us look instead at the various strata of
Maugham's life out of which the comedy was composed. The per-
nickety husband is a passionate collector of antique furniture like
the clients of Syrie. But this is not merely the drawing-room of an
antique collector; it is also the drawing-room of a rising politician
whose mother eloped with a man of political promise in her generation. Maugham is thinking back to his visits to people like the Allhusens in Stoke Poges where he met the young Winston Churchill
who, unlike Lord Porteous, did years later become Prime Minister,
and did have it in his power to give away India.

And what of Lord Porteous's mistress, the elderly heroine of the
comedy, a lady whose raddled vitality eclipses the presence of everyone else? We have noted that Lily Langtry passed fleetingly through
Maugham's childhood on the plage at Deauville. As a man he met
her again when his affair with Sue was at its height on the liner
going to New York to attend the rehearsals of *The Land of Promise*.
She reminisced about some of her illustrious lovers and when they
reached New York she told him she went to dance halls and danced
with the professional gigolos. Maugham pays a tribute to the era
of Jersey Lily in one of the most effective scenes in *The Circle* when
Lady Kitty turns the pages of an old photo album noting the exquisite plates of the great Edwardian beauties and their beaux while
not recognizing the loveliest of them all, herself. Here Maugham
was also thinking back to the *elegantes* of the British Embassy in
Paris and the photograph by his bedside.

While indulging such unabashed nostalgia Maugham makes
Lady Kitty talk very astutely to the young wife, who is on the brink
of bolting, about the economic consequences of such an action; she
reminds her that outside a marriage a woman has no status and that
if she has no money of her own she becomes a mere chattel of the
man she has eloped with. Syrie's increasing renown in her career
caused Maugham to ponder women's lib. long before that phrase
became current, and to make it the main subject of a later comedy,
The Constant Wife. In this one just when the audience thinks he
has finally settled for the hard line he pulls out the romantic stop
and permits the young lovers to borrow Lord Porteous's car as they
start their flit to San Michele (encapsulating yet another layer of
Maugham's life).

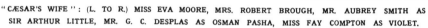

"CÆSAR'S WIFE" : (L. TO R.) MISS EVA MOORE, MRS. ROBERT BROUGH, MR. AUBREY SMITH AS SIR ARTHUR LITTLE, MR. G. C. DESPLAS AS OSMAN PASHA, MISS FAY COMPTON AS VIOLET.

THE LOVERS : MR. GEORGE RELPH AS RONALD PARRY AND MISS FAY COMPTON AS LADY LITTLE.

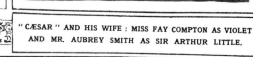

"CÆSAR" AND HIS WIFE : MISS FAY COMPTON AS VIOLET AND MR. AUBREY SMITH AS SIR ARTHUR LITTLE.

RIGHT
Pioneer of Women's Lib: Fay Compton
with Leon Quartermain in *The Constant
Wife*.

OPPOSITE
Advice from a bolter: Lottie Venne
left and Fay Compton in *The Circle*,
1921.

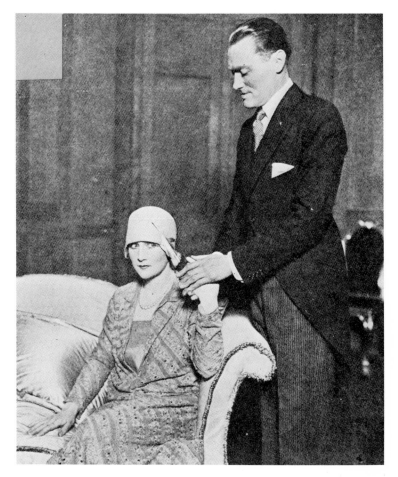

This perpetual alternation in the play between a realistic and a
romantic view of life, between the voice of youth and the voice of
experience, is what gives the comedy its peculiar, beguiling magic –
but it is also an expression of Maugham's own nature. He was the
least committed of writers in that he always kept his options open.
Maugham does not either commend or condemn Strickland, neither
does he either commend or condemn the lovers here. Instead he
provides us with a balancing act.

Unfortunately for Maugham he was not nearly so successful in
sustaining his equilibrium in the balancing act of his own life at
this time. Here again he kept his options open with Syrie at home
and Gerald abroad, but even if he were prepared to pivot himself
in the middle, neither of them was happy as a counterweight to the
other, inevitably a fight for sole possession occurred, as Beverley
Nichols has pointed out in *A Case of Human Bondage*. And when

it came to the crunch it was always Gerald who in Maugham's eyes tipped the balance heavily. The progress of the young American was already notorious. In 1916 he was up on a charge of gross indecency in London because of an incident that had occurred in a Covent Garden hotel. Haxton had been acquitted but at the same time had been declared an undesirable alien. Henceforth he was not permitted to set foot on English soil in spite of all Maugham's efforts to have the ban rescinded.

The banishment of Gerald from these shores served to heighten Maugham's desire, strong already for professional reasons, to spend long periods away from home in foreign travel. As soon as he had finished a book or a play he was impatient to pack his bags and rejoin his indispensable secretary-companion-general-factotum.

Their first major tour was in China in 1920. Even though the country was under a military dictatorship after the overthrow of the Ching dynasty, the Englishman and the American were able to wander around at will. Maugham took his usual quota of notes with the intention of working them up into another travel book, but when he read them later he decided to publish them just as they stood, brief, disconnected, but pristine. Or so he tells us in the preface to *On a Chinese Screen*, some of which was serialized in the *American Bookman* before appearing in bound form. I suspect, however, that he polished the notes pretty thoroughly. They seem just a little too neat and telling to be entirely off the cuff. Sir Harold Acton, Maugham's friend who was out in China at a slightly later time, admired the portraits in the book of several people he knew, especially the sage whom Maugham depicts as the Philosopher. Maugham travelled for five days by sampan to reach the Upper Yangtse to find him; as with so many of the different types of people Maugham met in the country he did not conform to the preconceived notions Maugham had formed of oriental patience and resignation. He was rather a tetchy and ebullient individual. Regarding himself as the last representative of the Old China he launched into a vehement attack upon the revolution and he concluded the interview by courteously presenting Maugham with two of his poems copied out in his own calligraphic hand. When translated by a Chinese-speaking friend they emerged as poems of disillusion in love very much to Maugham's taste.

Sir Harold told me that Maugham was very pleased with his description of the Great Wall of China and he would read it aloud

claiming that it was just as good, if not better, than the prose of
Virginia Woolf and other fashionable writers among the intelligentsia. I would not myself advance Maugham's Wall in support
of the claim that he has been seriously underrated as writer of descriptive prose. I would prefer to find some exotic scene from *The
Narrow Corner* or some English landscape from *Cakes and Ale*, but
I would commend the little China book as a whole as an unjustly
neglected work of which he was rightly rather proud.

In addition the journey also provided him with material for a
novel and a play. The latter was entitled *East of Suez* and was set –
very expensively set – in Peking. Within its oriental trappings it told
of a disastrous inter-racial love-affair and it was produced by the
young director Basil Dean at His Majesty's Theatre in September
1922 with Henry Kendall, Basil Rathbone and Meggie Albanesi.
It must be one of the least revived of Maugham's plays and it is
perhaps only memorable for the fact that the twangy music for it
was specially composed by Eugene Goosens who toured London's
Limehouse for some music to copy.

On the other hand the novel, *The Painted Veil*, has had a popular
success both as a book and a movie which harsher critics consider
out of all proportion to its merit. It was set in Hong Kong and tells
how an erring wife was sent by her husband to accompany him on
a lethal mission to a plague-spot where working to alleviate distress
with a community of nuns she discovers a more authentic kind of
life than she has known hitherto. Here I uphold the popular verdict
and persist in regarding it as a fine novel, anticipating works like
The Heart of the Matter by Graham Greene.

It ran into all sorts of libel difficulties on publication. When it
was being serialized in *Nash's Magazine* before book-publication
the names of the main characters had to be changed and then after
the review copies had gone out to the press all references to Hong
Kong and its environs had to be altered after angry representations
by the Assistant Secretary of the Hong Kong Government. Years
later when all the fuss had died away the name of Hong Kong was
reinstated throughout and appears as such in the modern paperback
edition you are likely to buy at a bookstall, but if by chance you
should come across a dilapidated hardback dated 1925 with Hong
Kong as the setting, snap it up. It could be worth a small fortune
to collectors of Maugham rarities. As he acidly remarked at the time,
several of the review copies were not returned to the publishers as
requested.

East of Suez, 1922, with Basil Rathbone, Meggie Albanesi, Marie Ault, Malcolm Keene and C.V. France.

Certainly Maugham did not endear himself to his Anglo-Saxon hosts when they read the novels and stories that appeared in the wake of the hospitality they had provided for him and his companion. Many were the pink colonial gorges that rose after publication day, vehement the fulminations against the vicious literary viper they had clasped so unsuspectingly to their bosoms. This inevitable reaction did not deter Maugham and Haxton from undertaking further journeys throughout the East. Two years after they returned from China they went to the Federated Malay States, Borneo and Sarawak, and in the following year to Burma. That produced a more discursively written travelogue, *The Gentleman in the Parlour*, sub-titled 'a record of a journey from Rangoon to Haiphong'; it was the visit to the FMS that inspired one of Maugham's best-known stories, 'The Letter'.

This story particularly gave grave offence to the locals, because it acquired even greater popularity in its dramatized form with Gladys Cooper, who inaugurated her career as an actress-manageress at the Playhouse with it. One member of the colonial service who was serving in the East at this time, Victor Purcell, wrote in his autobiography that Maugham's 'passage was clearly marked by a trail of angry people. The indignation aroused by his play *The Letter* which was based on a local *cause célèbre* was still being voiced in emotional terms when I came by.' Here again recent scholarship enables one to identify the historical originals from whom Maugham took the story of Leslie Crosbie, the wife of a rubber-planter, who during the absence of her husband in Singapore one night, shoots another white man dead whom she says was attempting to rape her.

The detective work has in this case been carried out by Professor Norman Sherry who disclosed his findings in an article published in *The Observer Colour Magazine* on 22 February 1976, 'How murder on the veranda inspired Somerset Maugham.' The trauma suffered by the white community over the original scandal was so deep that Sherry some fifty years later was still able to find one person in the Ai Hou Kee bar in Singapore who remembered it. However, it was only when he worked patiently back through the files of the *Straits Times* and the *Malay Mail* that the full story emerged. Maugham was resurrecting a scandal that happened in Kuala Lumpur many years before. 'According to these reports,' writes Sherry, 'a Mrs Ethel Mabel Proudlock, wife of the acting head of the Victoria Institution in Kuala Lumpur (a famous school still in existence), shot on the veranda of her home a Mr William

Crozier Steward, manager of a tin-mine. The parallels with Maugham's story were remarkable.'

One of these was the fact – the only incontrovertible fact in the story – that the murdered man was shot not once but six times. Maugham's heroine, thanks to the corruptibility of a Chinese law clerk, gets away with the killing and is acquitted. Mrs Proudlock was not acquitted. The prosecution alleged that Steward had visited her by arrangement and that he had been living with a Chinese woman. In the face of this Mrs Proudlock was judged to be guilty and sentenced to be hanged. Both her compatriots and leading members of the Chinese community petitioned the Sultan of Selangor for a free pardon on the grounds that she had 'received great provocation and acted as she did only for the protection of her honour'. Even though she herself withdrew her appeal she was in the end granted a pardon by the Sultan and returned home to England later to die in an asylum.

Once again life appears to have presented Maugham with his story on a plate. In fact, as Sherry finally shows, he got wind of it through his host and hostess in Singapore, a Mr and Mrs Courtenay Dickinson. He was a well-known lawyer there and she an equally celebrated hostess, famous for her gin cocktails. They appear in the story under the name of Joyce. It was he who told Maugham about the case and Maugham appeared 'very interested'.

'The Letter' is the last of the six stories in *The Casuarina Tree* (1926). The one before it, 'The Yellow Streak', is interesting in showing Maugham using something that happened to him while he was on his travels as the main episode of a story, while making it serve a completely different development of character and theme than the one offered by life. As he put it in a postscript to the volume, somewhat disingenuously: 'I venture to claim that the persons of these stories are imaginary, but since an incident in one of them, "The Yellow Streak", was suggested by a misadventure of my own, I wish more particularly to state that no reference is intended to either of my companions on that hazardous occasion.'

'The hazardous occasion' almost cost both Maugham and Haxton their lives. It was when they were travelling up the Sarawak River in Borneo to observe the life of the Dyak people. They suddenly found themselves engulfed by a dangerous tidal phenomenon known as the Bore. Huge waves made havoc of their boat which started to spin like a wheel. The travellers were tipped out and had to swim for the shore. Maugham was weakened during the long

tough haul to safety, Gerald stayed by him, giving him a hand and shouting encouragement. Finally one of the natives in the crew made a life-belt out of some blanket that was floating around the boat. Maugham clung on to it and with its help managed to swim to the shore with Gerald. They both scrambled on to the bank covered in mud where Gerald, suffering perhaps from excessive in-take of alcohol, had a heart attack. Maugham stayed helplessly by him thinking he was dying until after an hour they were both picked up and taken to the Dyak long-house where they were due to stay the night.

If you compare the factual description of this episode in Maugham's *Notebook* with the use of it in 'The Yellow Streak' you will not find much substantial difference between the two accounts, but in the *Notebook* Maugham tries to analyse the effect of it on his own character, revealing how the physical exertion prevented him from feeling afraid, whereas in the story he makes one of the two men involved suffer a failure of nerve and spend the rest of the week trying to cover-up his cowardice; at the end Maugham reveals that though seemingly white he is of mixed blood. Not that the collection as a whole presents the white settler in any very flattering light. If a yellow streak betrays mixed blood, the British administration is shown to consist of alcoholics, murderesses, tyrants, cowards, adulterers. In awarding this collection a place in his hundred key books of The Modern Movement, Cyril Connolly said that Maugham was the first writer to show 'exactly what the British in the Far East were really like', which is perhaps only another way of saying they were human. To judge from recent accounts of life in these parts their successors are not much of an improvement.

9

The Villa Mauresque

Driving along the corniche from Villefranche to Beaulieu-sur-mer you pass on your right a peninsula jutting out into the Mediterranean known as St Jean Cap Ferrat. Today the pleasant region is open to anyone with a bulging enough bill-folder of French francs, but once it was the exclusive preserve of Leopold II, King of the Belgians. He built himself a palace there as well as organizing residences for the different members of his entourage including separate houses for each of his three mistresses and a plot of land for his confessor, a retired bishop who had spent most of his working life in Algeria. This elderly ecclesiastic built a villa on it in the Moorish style with cupola and colonnades to which he had become accustomed. The villa stood in its own spacious grounds with a fine view of the sea and came to be known as the Villa Mauresque, eventually just as the Mauresque.

In 1928 it was purchased by Somerset Maugham who employed an architect to redesign it drastically. An essential feature of the new plan was a rooftop writing-room remote from the rest of the house. Maugham had decided that he must have a villa of his own away from England where he could live and write when he returned from his travels and which he could share with Gerald. Maugham's marriage had failed in spite of desperate eleventh-hour efforts by Syrie to save it: she had even gone so far as to purchase a villa herself in Le Touquet decorated in her most exquisite white in which she had hoped vainly that it might be possible for all three of them to live together.

Such a solution was clearly doomed from the start given the temperaments of the three people involved and as soon as Maugham had removed himself to the Mauresque she settled for a divorce which was arranged fairly amicably. Meanwhile Maugham began the task of hanging the pictures he had acquired on the walls of his new house and of establishing there that rigorous routine of

OPPOSITE
Maugham and Syrie before they
separated.

writing which he would let nothing interrupt. It was not at first quite the magnificent residence it later became with swimming pool and tennis court; the garden, one of its glories was the outcome of twenty-five years' work by Maugham's later secretary, Alan Searle. The whole place was razed to the ground by developers after Maugham's death. In the heyday of the Mauresque one American visitor is said to have remarked after walking around the garden and inspecting the Villa with its Renoirs, Matisses, Gauguin, Wilson Steers, Bonnard, Monet, Marie Laurencins, Picassos (not to mention the O'Conors going back to the days of the Chat Noir), 'All this – out of books!'

I never went there but I have talked to those who did and found them unanimous in praise of the discreet charm with which they were entertained. Maugham was a perfect if somewhat astringent host. Breakfast would be served on a tray in your room and for the remainder of the morning you would be at liberty to wander anywhere with the exception of the writing-room. At about half-past twelve the Master (that term begins to become current for Maugham now at first as a kind of joke, later acquiring a nuance of the French *maître*) would appear, his day's work behind him. Drinks would then be served by the butler on the terrace before lunch which would be a fairly relaxed informal occasion. After it was over you might decide to swim or play tennis while Maugham disappeared for his afternoon rest. At half-past six or so you would go into the drawing-room dressed for dinner where Maugham would partake of his Martini mixed for him by Haxton, an expert in the preparation of this mystical drink, knowing to perfection how to give it just the right degree of chill, the merest tincture of vermouth blending harmoniously with the deep groundswell of gin. Dinner would reveal the skill of the chef and the standards of the food to the full; none of the dishes would ever be repeated during the course of your stay.

Combined with these gastronomic delights there would be those of your host's conversation. The flow of talk would continue after dinner, interrupted perhaps by a rubber of bridge or a game of backgammon until bedtime. The Master, bidding you a formal goodnight, would prepare to turn his mind relaxingly to the latest thriller by Agatha Christie or Raymond Chandler.

Maugham liked to tease and to probe. He liked to put you on the spot and in all your various exchanges with him you would tend to come off the worse. Something of the flow of his talk as it might

Two paintings from Maugham's collection: *above* 'Still Life with Bowl of Apples' by Roderic O'Conor, 1923 and *opposite* 'Femme à l'ombrelle vert' by Henri Matisse, 1920.

switch from the lightning appraisal of a fellow-writer to the more general consideration of the supremacy of form in art, or the Russian sense of humour, or the psychology of a murderer or whatever, has been preserved for posterity by the American film director and play-wright, Garson Kanin, in his book, *Remembering Mr Maugham*. Kanin and his wife, Ruth Gordon, the actress, were but two among hundreds of distinguished guests who stayed at the villa during Maugham's long occupancy of it. Among these were the grand friends of the Master, people like the Duke and Duchess of Windsor, Aga Khan, Lord Beaverbrook, Sir Winston Churchill, Lord Boothby and other members of the British aristocracy whom he knew well. There is a legendary story of how at the time of the abdication crisis, Mrs Simpson, as she then was, partnering the Master at bridge, suffered a rebuke for failing to call higher when

she had a king in her hand. She is supposed to have said: 'It is supported only by knaves and a king is useless when surrounded only by knaves.'

Then there were visits from authors – Kipling, H.G. Wells, Elizabeth Russell, about each of whom Maugham published reminiscences; more frequent guests than these would be a fashionable circle of writers of lesser talent and fame than he, unashamedly aiming at the popular audience, true believers in his gospel of steady unremitting work every day including Sundays, birthdays and Christmas. Among them one must include Beverley Nichols, Godfrey Winn, G.B. Stern, and Noël Coward, more a rival than a disciple, operating from a comparable base of reputation and wealth. 'They were like two panthers prowling cautiously around each other,' commented an observer.

Certainly Maugham did not wish to be surrounded by flatterers and imitators. He loved to pit his strength against the expert, the authority, the scholar, the cultivated and discriminating mind. Other regular guests over the years were people like Lord and Lady Clark, Arthur Marshall and George Rylands of King's College, Cambridge. Lord Clark recalls that while he was staying with him Maugham,

talked a lot about literature and he even talked occasionally about what he was writing and he even, which I consider a very great compliment, used to show me certain passages and ask my opinion about how certain phrases should be altered or what words should be chosen. He was a very very conscientious craftsman and he was prepared to do anything to get it right.

George Rylands whom Maugham once persuaded to give him a tutorial as if he were some first year student at Cambridge says,

the nicest time was simply sitting with him either on the terrace with a drink before luncheon or in the evening and talking about books from various points of view. He thought of me of course as rather a don and academic – or pretended so to think and teased me. He knew I was also very interested in drama and had produced plays and myself was a very keen amateur actor. We talked about that and we talked about Hazlitt. I remember our talking a lot about Hazlitt and also he had a very high opinion of Dryden's style, quite rightly, and we discussed that.

Finally there were hordes of what one might call visiting firemen, fellow-writers *en route* in the south of France whom he would entertain for lunch or drinks, and this would include both the stalwart professional and the unknown beginner. Frank Swinnerton recalls going to the Mauresque with his wife. They were treated impeccably but felt something sinister in the air and were glad to leave. Arthur Marshall remembers one occasion when he was staying away in Monte Carlo and Maugham suddenly said after dinner at about eleven o'clock: 'Gentlemen, a choice awaits you. Either you can leave now by car. Or you will have to w-w-alk.' C.P. Snow, just after he had published his first book which had only sold a minimal number of copies, recalls seeing Maugham who was encouraging, telling him that this was more copies than his first book had sold and next time he might hope for something 'be-better'. Young Frederic Raphael, winner of the Somerest Maugham award which the Master endowed to enable a young writer to spend a few months in uninterrupted travel, also recalls an encouraging visit to the Mauresque after the Second World War.

In fact the villa became one of the great places of pilgrimage on the Mediterranean for those who cultivate the arts, the other main ones being Max Beerbohm's villa at Rapallo, and those of Bernard Berenson and Harold Acton near Florence.

Henry James speaks somewhere of a writer's concentration as a fortress that must brook no defeat from the private self as it so easily might. Maugham agreed with that view implicitly. Every morning until luncheon he pulled up the drawbridge, so to speak. A book a year – sometimes more than a book a year – became his norm; there appeared to be nothing to which he could not successfully turn his hand, whether it was fiction, short or long, travel or literary essay, comedy or drama in the theatre. Only verse – there is one highly embarrassing poem probably to Haxton extant in the Notebook – remained unattempted.

Such a degree of professional competence – to put it no higher than that – naturally produced a backlash among reviewers and critics. Panning Somerset Maugham became a popular sport in the weeklies and Sundays. His detractors multiplied along with his fortune from royalties and subsidiary rights; indeed there is a direct correlation between the two. The gulf between Maugham and 'the intelligentsia' remained and hardened implacably, and has ossified since as I myself discovered a few years ago when I published a book suggesting that he had been underrated as an artist.

Bloomsbury and its values came more and more to dominate the London literary world, and Bloomsbury regarded Maugham's books as beyond their pale. 'Class II, Division I,' was Lytton Strachey's comment on *The Painted Veil* when he read it during a bout of flu. Only Virginia Woolf was gracious enough to give Harold Nicolson, on his way from Rodmell to Cap Ferrat, a message for Maugham saying that she had found *The Summing-Up* a wonderfully honest account of the life of a writer. It was not just Bloomsbury that had little time for Maugham. It was anyone who claimed to be trying to extend the frontiers of English fiction. D.H. Lawrence, for example, happened to be earning some money in the late 1920s by reviewing for the London *Vogue* and he pitched into the spy stories that Maugham published in 1928. Lawrence informed his readers:

Mr Ashenden is an elderly author [Maugham was in his early forties when he was being Ashenden, fifty-four by the time the stories appeared as a book] so he takes life seriously, and takes his fellow-men seriously, with

Maugham's circle: *above left* Robert Boothby; *above right* Beverley Nichols; *opposite left* Godfrey Winn; *opposite right* G.B. Stern.

a seriousness already a little out of date. He has a sense of responsibility towards humanity. It would be much better if he hadn't. For Mr Ashenden's sense of responsibility oddly enough is inverted. He is almost passionately concerned with proving that all men and all women are either dirty dogs or imbeciles. If they are clever men or women, they are crooks, spies, police-agents, and tricksters 'making good', living in the best hotels because they know that in a humble hotel they'll be utterly *déclassé*, and showing off their base cleverness and being dirty dogs, from Ashenden himself, and his mighty clever colonel, and the distinguished diplomat, down to the mean French porters.

Perhaps a non-combatant married to a German baroness was not the most receptive reviewer for Ashenden. The final wounding twist of the knife came in the last paragraph:

But these stories, being 'serious', are faked. Mr Maugham is a splendid observer. He can bring before us persons and places most excellently. But as soon as the excellently observed characters have to move, it is a fake. Mr Maugham gives them a humorous shove or two. We find they are nothing but puppets, instruments of the author's pet prejudice. The author's pet prejudice being 'humour' it would be hard to find a batch of more ill-humoured stories, in which the humour has gone more rancid.

This review came as a crescendo to a chorus that had been singing in Maugham's ears ever since he first began to publish his stories in volume form in 1921. He had had great trouble placing 'Miss Thompson' until eventually it was taken by H.L. Mencken and George Jean Nathan for *The Smart Set*, but from then on his stories found a ready market in both America and Britain. It was when they were collected about six at a time into books that they came under reviewers' fire. The first volume containing the South Sea Island stories, *The Trembling of a Leaf*, was reviewed by Rebecca West (whose early brilliance as a book-critic had been spotted by Violet Hunt and Ford Madox Ford), reviewing fiction for the *New Statesman*. She wrote of a 'certain cheap and tiresome attitude towards life, which nearly mars these technically admirable stories'. The cynicism, she claimed, was merely a cover-up for an inner emptiness: the admiration for the courage of the drop-out in 'The Fall of Edward Barnard' is cancelled out by the contempt for the drop-out in 'Red', leaving 'an impression of nothingness'. She did, though, have good words for 'Rain' and 'Mackintosh'.

Did Maugham mind these continual critical barbs? Did he care about his non-acceptance by the intellectuals? At the time he pretended not to mind. He talked of shrugging his shoulders and going his way. He wryly noted the fact that clever young men down from the university failed to write appreciative appraisals of his work, and commented: 'I must bear my misfortune with fortitude.' He could always console himself by purchasing another Bonnard or Marie Laurencin. Moreover he could look with satisfaction to the reception of his work in the United States and on the continent of Europe. In France and Germany his writing was already becoming the subject of academic study; critical accounts of his philosophy were beginning to appear. In France, his adopted land, some of his stories were translated by Gerald Haxton who counted fluent French among his other attributes.

But whatever outward show of indifference Maugham might adopt, inwardly in his writer's soul he minded very much about his rating in the eyes of the London literary world. The occasional dissentient voice, such as Desmond MacCarthy's, who spoke of him as the English Maupassant, was all the sweeter for its rarity. Maugham wanted not just the gushing uncritical admiration of silly women in luncheon clubs, but also the respect of his pro-

Maugham in a light-hearted mood in
1929 at the Villa Mauresque shortly
after he had purchased it.

fessional contemporaries, the approval of his peer-group. Which of
us does not?

Maugham's way of hitting back was always to do so through work.
He never wasted working-time writing letters to editors or reviewers. Instead he pondered creatively the whole question of how
literary reputations are made and sustained, or not sustained, in
London. Now that he had abandoned that city for good apart from
an annual summer visit spent at the Dorchester Hotel, he could
observe its literary mafia, its smart drawing-rooms, exclusive West

End Clubs and its whole crazy system of values in which social and literary success overlapped with a measure of detachment. He began to wonder whether this world could not itself become the subject for a story. Clearly it would have to be a work of fiction but one that gave an account of literary reputation-building as close to the reality as he could possibly go. The germ of the idea lay in the notion he had of a story about a famous writer who when completely unknown was living at Whitstable with a blowsy common wife and was ostracized by the gentry.

When he first thought of this Maugham was under contract to the American journal *Cosmopolitan Magazine*, edited by Ray Long, to write a story a month and he wondered whether his plot might not do for one of these. But they had to be very short indeed – they were eventually published in book form as *Cosmopolitans* – only about 1200–1500 words. (Long had admired the sketches in *On A Chinese Screen* and had asked Maugham to write fiction of the same length to give his readers a story they could devour entire on opposite pages of the magazine with an illustration.) What finally prevented Maugham from using his famous writer story in this way was the model he had at the back of his mind for the character of the wife. For a long time he had wanted to purge his memory of his lost love, Sue Jones, and she seemed in her voluptuous and promiscuous essence to be the ideal first wife for such a writer. But there was far too much of Sue to be confined to a mere fifteen hundred words.

A more complex work than a single short story began to emerge. It would deal both with his love life and with his literary life, both with his boyhood and with his early years in London; it would be by turns both nostalgic and satirical. Above all, it would be light-hearted; it would – *pace* D.H. Lawrence – have a sense of humour permeating its every word. Maugham hated self-appointed ruling cabals whether they governed literary fashion or moral conduct, and he proposed in the form of a novel to expose as fully as he could the workings of those cabals he had observed at close range. He recalled a remark from *Twelfth Night* when Sir Toby Belch asks of the repressive steward to whom he is such an unwelcome, verbose guest, 'Dost thou think, because thou art virtuous, there shall be no more cakes and ale?' The novel which Maugham published under that title in 1930 many people consider to be his masterpiece.

10

His House in Order

Throughout *Cakes and Ale* Maugham addresses us in the first person, speaking with sardonic candour of matters that intimately concern him. This air of confidentiality is of course an illusion, a stance that sharpens the satirical focus of the work; but it is true that in this novel Maugham is presenting us with a sequence of self-portraits more fully rounded than those in any of his other novels or stories except *Of Human Bondage*. He gives the narrator his own Christian name Willie, adding Ashenden, the surname of a schoolfriend at Canterbury which, as we have seen, he had used already for his spy stories. He took pleasure in the burnt-out case association in this name.

In the novel we observe Willie Ashenden at three distinct periods of his life: the young boy, the young man, the established author. The Willie Ashenden whom we meet at the opening is a modestly successful man of letters with lodgings in Half Moon Street in the heart of London near Piccadilly and Green Park. We gather from the first few pages that a vastly more successful and fashionable colleague, the novelist Alroy Kear, has telephoned him on a matter of some urgency, and that Ashenden is at a loss to discover why he should suddenly be sought after in this way.

When Maugham published his novel he was well into his fifties with a hugely successful career behind him (even though he still had a long way to go, being over ninety when he died). In 1930 Maugham was every bit as famous and successful as Alroy Kear. In Willie Ashenden we have a flashback to his situation some decades earlier when he had recently left medical school and was struggling to make his name as a novelist. Yet during the passages where Ashenden unburdens his mind to the reader, and he spends a lot of the book interrupting the narrative to do that, his utterances have the wisdom, the assurance, and the deep knowledge of literature as a profession of the mature Maugham.

An illustration by J. Sloan to the 1938 edition of *Of Human Bondage*: 'She had never looked so unattractive, but it was too late now.'

Maugham plays down his own success not merely out of modesty or English good taste, but because it is success in literature in England and therefore the significant part played by society and fashion in the making of a literary reputation, that lies at the heart of the novel. The writer is going to take us behind the scenes in the world of contemporary letters; it is essential to his tactics of exposing what goes on there that he at least should emerge as a sympathetic figure with whom the reader may identify. Ashenden's self-effacing reasonableness serves as a foil to Kear's self-importance, manoeuvring and deviousness. Maugham makes it clear that Kear possesses very little talent, about as much, we are informed, as 'a heaped-up tablespoon of Bemax' (a rather tasteless breakfast food with laxative properties). 'He was an example,' Maugham writes, 'of what an author can do, and to what heights he can rise, by industry, common sense, honesty, and the efficient combination of means and ends.'

The preliminary sketch of Kear, tracing his rise from a high-grade Civil Service and military family background to intimacy with the nobility and universal popularity among middle-class readers of fiction, is one of the cruellest portraits of one author by another in the whole of English literature. Alexander Pope was hardly more murderous in *The Dunciad* inspired by the same hatred of people he considered to be mediocrities elevated to a position of commanding eminence. In his Malayan stories we have seen how Maugham used real people as models for his fictional creations; here the model for Kear was the novelist Hugh Walpole (1884–1941), a friend of Maugham's, like him an alumnus of The King's School, Canterbury.

If Maugham deals harshly with Kear he is just as ruthless in his portrayal of the society of which Kear is the darling. Maugham shows us how the efficiently oiled inner wheels of the mechanism of success in literature are made to turn. He spotlights the manipulation of opinion by a self-appointed female-run cultural élite. This élite is controlled by Mrs Barton Trafford who 'takes up' an author just before he is becoming widely read and drops him, oh so gently, just after the fickle craze for his work has run its course. In her own well-bred way Mrs Trafford anticipates the methods of modern public relations. Her career as confidante and protectress of great men of letters reaches its climax when she attaches herself to Edward Driffield.

Driffield belongs to a type to which Maugham always felt akin, the man of natural genius who lives entirely within his own strength. Maugham believed that a genuine artist should always remain 'aloof' (the word is the key to Maugham's creed), aloof from society, aloof from his critics, aloof from his readers; Maugham was aloof, Gauguin was aloof, Driffield was aloof. Such aloofness implies a contempt for the current morality. Driffield's refusal to bow to the values of his time, those of Edwardian England, is shown in various ways and at different times in the narrative. The main model for him is Thomas Hardy, though Maugham never really knew Hardy at all well, the character owes his fun-loving buoyancy to Wells, and his rifling of the experience of his nearest and dearest to Maugham himself.

One day Driffield and Rosie 'shoot the moon', absconding from Blackstable with all their bills unpaid. This episode was suggested to Maugham by his memory of a spectacular local bankruptcy, and so was the character of 'Lord' George Kemp, whose ripe Edwardian panache was, as Robert H. Goodsall recalled in his *A Fourth Kentish Patchwork*, inspired by 'Harry Gann [the surname Maugham used for Rosie] a prominent townsman always immaculately turned out, debonnaire [sic], a flower in the buttonhole of his jacket, gaily twirling his walking-stick as he briskly strutted down the High Street, a character'.

It is the later Driffield after he has achieved eminence, the ruggedly grand old man of English literature, who most closely resembles Hardy in the first decades of the century. The presence of Driffield – Mr Goodsall discovered in the parish records that this surname belonged to one of Parson Maugham's churchwardens – is made to suffuse the whole novel even though we do not see all that much of him. His wink to Willie when they meet at a respectable luncheon party speaks volumes. He remains throughout alien to the world of Kear, Mrs Trafford, and of his own second wife, Amy. The tension between them is all the more effective for being presented in a light-hearted mood rather than a solemn one. Driffield is associated in Willie's memory with a vanished time of conviviality, fun and games; his first wife Rosie, the heroine of the story, and her bibulous paramour 'Lord' George serve to reveal this aspect of the great man. Between them they represent a 'set' of which the curate is a secret member. They are comparable to the riotous cronies who gather round the maid Maria in Shakespeare's play.

Here the forces of respectability are attempting to appropriate the memory of Driffield in the form of an official biography written by Kear at the behest of his second wife. They aim to perpetuate the legend by suppressing the facts of his chequered career as a young man in Blackstable, his marriage to a woman from what in those days would have been called 'the lower orders' ('The Skeleton In The Cupboard' of Maugham's subtitle to the novel). It so happens that thanks to his own Blackstable background Willie Ashenden is the only living witness of any consequence of Driffield's origins. The forces of respectability consider it wise to 'square' him before proceeding with their project.

In our period of obsessive candour in literary biography it is hard to imagine how such a plan could have worked, but even as recently as 1930 the suppression of awkward episodes in the official lives of great men was by no means uncommon. In the biography of Thomas Hardy, for instance, published in 1928, purporting to be written by his first wife, we receive a heavily censored view of the novelist and the book is now known to have been written by Hardy himself. Maugham with his keen nose for such things might well have been aware of this piece of pious fraud at an early stage conceiving from it the design of *Cakes and Ale*.

Be that as it may, this putative biography of Driffield provides Maugham with a most felicitous structural device for his novel, permitting him to range freely back and forth from present to past. An analysis of all the time-shifts in the novel is well outside of the scope of this book but the exercise would offer some insights into the mature technique of a writer who often referred to himself with humility as but a story-teller. The extreme cunning of the novel's construction matches the piquant irony of its tone; the mixture is one of finely balanced contrasts, past matches present, Driffield matches Kear, metropolitan London matches rural Blackstable, the narrator's urbanity matches his callow youth when he saw more than he fully comprehended.

In *Of Human Bondage* Maugham was exorcizing the traumas of his broken childhood. Now we see the more sunlit, happier, normal aspects of Maugham's formative years. Like any other boy Willie learns to ride a bicycle. The place where he practises and catches his first unforgettable sight of Rosie Gann is called Joy Lane. There happens to be a real lane of that name which may still be located on a map of the Whitstable region. Yet surely Maugham made Rosie and Driffield meet young Willie there with reason, seizing upon the actual name as expressing the mood of this part of the book. Is not Rosie the most magnificent of the English Edwardian *filles de joie*?

In her Maugham remembered the don juanism of his Pall Mall days *du côté de chez* Walter Payne. At these moments Maugham is hard pressed to sustain his urbanity and comes close to lapsing into sentimentality but he never quite loses his poise. By quoting the odious comments upon Rosie of Mrs Trafford and Amy Driffield he cleverly succeeds in having his cake and eating it, somehow presenting her at once as attractive and repulsive. The attention paid by Maugham to visual detail serves him particularly well in his depiction of Rosie; such a deft Flaubertian touch as the marks made upon her ample flesh by her tightly laced corset, when she takes it off before according Willie her final favours, brings a whole period flooding back. I would quote passages from *Cakes and Ale* to combat the oft-heard dismissal of Maugham's prose as being riddled with clichés. Here in scenes such as Willie's return to Blackstable and the interior of Rosie's bedroom it is the verbal counterpart to the work of contemporary English painters such as Sickert and Wilson Steer.

Yet if the surface of the book is polished and shimmering, it is in its penetration below the surface, its exposure of the attitudes governing respectable England that gives it, of all Maugham's work, its claim to a permanent place in our literature. Whether we are in London or in Blackstable, the same rules, the same pressures to conform, apply. The force of that pressure may be succinctly expressed by the word 'gentleman' which occurs so often through-out. It is a concept of repressive power whether upon a growing boy or a mature biographer. So far as we know Kear's biography of Driffield was never written, or if it was, it was soon forgotten: the definitive biography of Driffield remains *Cakes and Ale*.

The novel was published in September 1930 but the story of its reception really begins some weeks earlier when it was still at the page-proof stage. A set of proofs of *Cakes and Ale* were sent by Heinemann, the novel's British publisher, to the Book Society in the hope that it might become the Society's fiction choice. The Chairman of the Selection Committee was none other than Hugh Walpole who had first met Maugham in 1911 when he was begin-ning as a writer and Maugham was already established as a play-wright. Walpole had been to a theatre and had returned to his chambers in Half Moon Street (the same address as Ashenden in the book). He picked up the proof while half-undressed sitting on his bed, and began to read. 'Read on,' noted Walpole in his diary, 'with increasing horror. Unmistakable portrait of myself. Never

The first page of the manuscript for *Cakes and Ale*, 1930, which is now in the British Library.

slept.' In the small hours of the morning he rang A.S. Frere of Heinemann. Mr Frere still vividly recalls the chain of events:

He rang me up and said, Had I read the proofs of a book called *Cakes and Ale* which I was going to publish? And I said, Yes, and he said, Well, you can't publish it, and I said, Why not?, and he said, Well its outrageous, everything's wrong. Anyway, he didn't get very far. He said,

Come to lunch at the Reform Club. Because the Garrick was shut. We went to the Reform Club, and we met Frank Swinnerton and Arnold Bennett and one or two other characters like that. And all hell broke loose. Hugh was rushing around saying it was all about him and had better be stopped.

Well, Jack Priestley [J.B. Priestley] who was also on the Committee had also read it, and he came round to the office in the afternoon and said, Look here, we've got to convince Hugh that it isn't him, but that its John Drinkwater, and so we set about that operation and Hugh was eventually persuaded not to do anything about it. Willie, all that time had gone off somewhere round Singapore way, you know.

Walpole had not in the least been persuaded that Kear was based

'We've got to convince Hugh that it isn't him, but that it's John Drinkwater ...' Hugh Walpole *left* with J.B. Priestley in 1930.

on Drinkwater, as is apparent from Rupert Hart-Davis's biography, *Hugh Walpole: A Portrait of A Man, An Epoch and A Society*. The wound lingered, poisoning the remainder of his life even though towards the end of it he and Maugham were reconciled. Maugham's part in the whole affair was inexcusable unless you believe that all's fair in love and literature. He began by denying the impeachment in a private letter to Walpole. The portrait of Kear, he declared, was a composite one. He had borrowed traits from a great many different writers, not the least from himself. And Maugham kept up this pretence in a preface to the book only eventually admitting the truth in 1950 after Walpole's death in an introduction to the New York Modern Library edition.

What was particularly galling to Walpole because it touched a nerve of truth was the novel's description of Kear's way of dealing with hostile reviews by taking the authors of them out to lunch at his club and through his ingratiating behaviour making sure that the review of the next book was couched in much more friendly tones. Walpole found a champion in the American novelist Elinor Mordaunt to his considerable embarrassment. She came up with a riposte to *Cakes and Ale* in the form of a novel called *Gin and Bitters* set partly in the South Seas, purporting to give an accurate account of Maugham's travels. It is a feeble effort because although she knew the setting she did not really know her man. Martin Secker tried to publish it in England in 1931, but under threat of legal action by Maugham (with the encouragement of Walpole, oddly, who feared people might think Elinor Mordaunt was a pseudonym of his) he was forced to withdraw the book. However it did anonymously appear in the United States. Raymond Toole Stott in his *A Bibliography of the Works of Somerset Maugham* (1973) interestingly reveals that Elinor Mordaunt was a close friend of the second Mrs Hardy.

Cakes and Ale is a classic instance of the revenge mechanism prompting Maugham to one of his finest pieces of writing. Ashenden was clever at spotting traitors because he was himself an arch-traitor. Most novelists are in fact traitors but not quite so blatantly as Maugham. Here he had taken the lid off a society of which he had been an aloof member. And Maugham did it again in 1937 about another world which he had come to know intimately, in a novel called *Theatre*. The sacred monsters of the stage were sitting ducks for Maugham; he waited until he was well clear of them professionally before he took a shot at them. The ghost of Marie

Tempest and other glittering ladies who had helped to make his plays so successful hovers over Julia Lambert, the heroine of this novel, who proves to be an even greater actress off the stage than she is on it. Maugham has some typically cruel fun at her expense while describing her amours, at the same time pondering a question that always fascinated him, the nature of artistic illusion.

By now he had become thoroughly disillusioned with the theatre as a repository for his own creative gift and in the early 1930s he bowed himself out of it as a practising playwright. As a theatregoer however, his interest remained until very near the end of his life. During their annual visits to London he and Alan Searle would always attend several theatres and he followed the career of a play-wright in the English realistic tradition like Terence Rattigan with interest. But he reckoned that play-writing was essentially a young man's job and at more than fifty it was time for him to quit before the public became tired of him.

Maugham phased himself out of the theatre with four plays that he said he wrote regardless of their chance of commercial success although at least two of them have proved to be among his most popular works. One, *The Sacred Flame*, was inspired by a family tragedy. Maugham's brother Charles – the one who had gone into the family law firm in Paris and married the painter 'Beldy' – had three daughters and one son whom he called Ormond after his own father. This boy fell from a tree at school and was paralysed for the rest of his life. Maugham had observed the mother's devotion to her crippled son and conceived of the awful dramatic idea of a mercy-killing, thus providing Gladys Cooper with two of her most memorable roles; first as Stella, the son's wife, in the original production of 1928, and then later as Mrs Tarbert, the mother.

After this sombre piece he wrote a comedy about a stockbroker who discovers late in the day à la Gauguin that life is for living, *The Breadwinner* (1930); a searing drama about post-war England and the fate of the ex-servicemen, *For Services Rendered* (1932); and a comedy based on one of his earliest stories about a London barber who on winning the Irish sweep tries to emulate Christ's teaching and give away all his new-found wealth to the poor and the needy, *Sheppey* (1933). As a kind of farewell gesture to the boards Maugham tried a little experiment here; he made the prosti-tute whom the barber befriends also symbolize his death. She greets him in the last act with the 'appointment in Samarra' story from the Arabian Nights. The scene was a flop. 'I do not think,' said

Maugham and Haxton having lunch with friends in Austria before the War.

Maugham, 'I was asking an audience to accept too much when I set before them an hallucination of Sheppey's disordered brain.' Terence Rattigan, who attended the first night, lays the blame squarely with Maugham.

I can assure you that the first night audience did accept it. There were great screams and cheers at the final curtain after a very, I thought, embarrassing scene with Laura Cowie playing both the tart and the death-figure at the end. I don't think he brought it off, frankly. I don't think he convinced the audience. He could . . . the audience was only too ready to accept it as the new experimental theatre but for me he didn't bring it off. What he did bring off in that same play was a marvellous performance by Angela Baddeley as the barber's daughter . . . I remember Angela running around the stage saying, 'Oh God, make him potty! Oh God, make him potty!' Very brave, I thought, and very good.

Rattigan's first great hit, *French Without Tears*, came on in 1936 three years after *Sheppey*, Maugham's last first night. By then Maugham's plays had begun to appear in a collected edition. Inside the copy he presented to Rattigan, Maugham wrote the following valedictory dedication: 'For Terry. The nostalgic day before yesterday (Noel) to the brilliant present. W. S. Maugham.' That was in 1946.

The English do not honour their writers as much as the Latin races, but in each generation they pick on one or two authors to serve as representatives for literature. Maugham came to fulfil this role in the latter days of the British Empire as Kipling had done before him. And, like Kipling, his main output went from now on into the short story.

Collections of stories by Maugham appeared at intervals throughout the decade – *Six Stories Written in the First Person Singular* (1931), *Ah King* (1933), *Cosmopolitans* (1933), *The Mixture as Before* (1940). The title of the last-named was taken from the heading to a review of one of the previous collections. It was Maugham's defiant riposte to the imputation that he had merely settled down to a formula. It is true that whether he was writing to a length of twelve thousand or merely one thousand words he insisted upon there being a beginning, a middle and an end, and that by the time that end was reached all reasonable curiosity about the main characters on the part of the reader had to be entirely satisfied. But within these canons Maugham's range is wide and varied. He continued in the *Ah King* volume to contribute to the literature of colonial experience, going back to Malaya with Haxton and finding fresh themes there as unflattering to the administration as the earlier ones. Consider the murderous couple who go scot-free in 'Footprints in the Jungle' or the unnaturally possessive passion of a sister for her brother in 'The Book Bag'.

At the same time Maugham cast his net along his now native Riviera coastline in stories like 'Gigolo and Gigolette' and 'The Three Fat Women of Antibes' and in the fashionable drawing-rooms of London in 'Lord Mountdrago' and 'Alien Corn'. In the latter story we see his art at its most accomplished tackling several of his favourite themes. First he presents what you may call a racial mask, in this instance of a wealthy Jewish family whose members have become more English than the English – riding to hounds and sending their sons to Eton. Against this background he places another favourite Maugham notion, the drop-out, the non-conformer, here a favourite son who wants to break with family tradition and become a musician, and this choice of profession gives Maugham his third theme: the need for the artist to prove himself and to win the approval of his peers. How cunningly Maugham makes these three subjects inter-act as he shows us the adopted manner of English understatement give way to innate Jewish demonstrativeness and family opposition turn into family solidarity as the would-be artist's hopes are dashed by the bitter evidence of failure.

Perhaps of all Maugham's themes, that of the world well lost is the most persistent. To his harassed readers throughout the economic depression of the 1930s it had a peculiarly telling appeal. Many were the city stockbrokers seeing Charles Battle jump on his silk hat in *The Breadwinner* who murmured under their breath: 'There but for the grace of God . . .'; many were the Sunday painters reading *The Moon and Sixpence* who thought to themselves *pourquoi pas moi* (why not me?). There is one recorded case of a highly successful individual who really did chuck it all up at over fifty to go to the South Seas and paint as a result of reading Maugham. This was the American Ray Long, the editor of *Cosmopolitan Magazine*, the man who encouraged Maugham to write those very short, short stories. Unfortunately Long's efforts as a painter were not crowned with success and he died by his own hand.

We are so used to thinking of Maugham as a master of realism that it comes as a surprise to note that at least two of his stories are written in a fanciful style, both containing his more considered thoughts on the subject of sexual passion. The one known as 'Princess September' (originally 'The Princess and the Nightingale') can be read like the *Happy Prince* of Oscar Wilde as a tale for children. Indeed it was based upon a story Maugham told his own daughter Liza, written originally for inclusion in the manuscript of the *Queen's Doll's House Library*, to which eminent men of letters were invited to contribute in their own hand. Afterwards it was published in 1924 in *The Book of the Queen's Doll's House Library* edited by E.V. Lucas. But it is also a story about the imprisoning effect of exclusive love.

In 'The Judgment Seat' published ten years later Maugham imagines a trio of respectable English people, two women and a man, killed in the war, who against all their natural instincts behaved well in the sense that they remained chaste within the Christian conception of marriage – the man resists an affair with the woman he loves passionately, and remains faithful to his wife, the other woman sublimates her passion in good works. All three wait expectantly for their reward in heaven. The Almighty blows upon them and they cease to exist. It is a queer, heartless little joke.

Maugham's perception of the destructive nature of possessive

Gerald Kelly painted eighteen different portraits of his friend Somerset Maugham, fifteen of which are now in the Humanities Research Centre of the University of Texas at Austin. Here are a selection from them showing the writer in different stages of his life: *below left* 1913; *right* 1932; *below right* 1935; *opposite left* 1953; *opposite right* 1963.

love does not appear to have made him personally more moderate in his own attachments to judge from accounts of those closest to him. His great passion Haxton was someone who could be relied upon to behave outrageously. His gambling debts were huge and it was inevitably Maugham who paid them. But when he did have a lucky touch he could be enchantingly convivial. Lady Kelly happily remembers one Riviera party on which he spent his entire winnings of a thousand pounds. Arthur Marshall recalls another occasion at the Mauresque waiting among a number of guests including several women for Maugham to come down for dinner; Mr Marshall observed Gerald pour himself out a full tumbler of neat gin which he downed at a gulp. Eventually Maugham made his belated

appearance apologizing and explaining that he had lingered in a hot bath. 'And did you masturbate?' asked Gerald. But then, as Mr Marshall says, Maugham expected people to behave badly and he was disappointed when they did not. In this respect Gerald rarely let him down.

They continued their travels around the globe until the outbreak of war. A trip to the Dutch East Indies provided in Banda-Neira the haunting setting for the novel *The Narrow Corner* where it appears as Kanda. Several visits to Spain, where Maugham always loved to go, resulted in a superb book, *Don Fernando* (1935), his own favourite among his works, combining insights into the great figures of Spanish civilization – Loyola, El Greco, Velasquez, Tirso de Molina, Cervantes – with impressions of the cities and the countryside. The narrative takes the form of a private quest for the truth about the face of a monk seen in a picture by Zurbaran.

Another year Maugham explored the Caribbean. This was the result of a suggestion he had had from Kipling, who had stayed with him at the Mauresque, that he would find wonderful material for stories there. But the place failed to spark his inspiration any more than it had Kipling's.

The place where he did find some good copy of a grim kind was French Guiana in the penal colony at Cayenne. Haxton explained to the Governor that the *cher mâitre* was very interested in the psychology of men undergoing long spells of captivity for serious crimes including murder, and everything was put at their disposal, including two murderers to wait on them. Maugham described this little excursion into Dostoyevsky country as 'a horrifying experience' but out of it he gathered the background for parts of the novel *Christmas Holiday* (1939) based upon a sensational murder trial in Paris before the war; in this novel the drop-out figure is an adolescent English public schoolboy who is brought to a realization of the ideological realities of a Europe about to explode.

As war became more and more inevitable Maugham's wanderlust took him away from Europe to the country Kipling had made his own, fictionally speaking. Maugham had been reluctant to broach territory upon which a fellow-author had so powerfully stamped his image, but when Maugham finally got to India in the late 1930s he found an India much to his taste. As well as all the Maharajahs and Princes to whom his friend the Aga Khan had provided him with introductions, and by whom he was munificently entertained (only the British administration jibbed at the presence of Haxton at some of the official receptions) Maugham also met yogis, mystics, scholars, poets and men of learning. He was particularly impressed by one swami whose ashram he visited at a place called Tiruvannah a few hours away by car from Madras at the foot of the mountain Arunchala. Maugham took a basket of fruit with him to present to the holy man. The route to the mountain hermitage was along an exceptionally hot and dusty track and by the time Maugham arrived he passed out with exhaustion. This was later reported as the famous author having been overcome by the aura of holiness. Not only did his visit give Maugham a centrepiece for his novel *The Razor's Edge*, he also wrote a long essay about the religious teacher in question who was known as the Maharishi.

As Maugham entered his sixties the mood came upon him of desiring to put his house in order. He still had several short stories and novels he wanted to write but before that he felt obliged to set down his considered thoughts upon some questions about the meaning of truth, beauty, and goodness, questions which most people have shrugged aside as beyond their capacity by the time they have reached a mature age. Maugham continued to worry away at them. From now on in his work we find the magic of the sorcerer who hooks you with his brilliantly naturalistic illusions combining with the industry of the apprentice who sits at the feet of the great minds – the great writers, philosophers and painters – while trying to make up his own. The book in which he brought together all his considerable efforts to make up his mind on the ultimate questions, hitherto scattered in various prefaces, travel essays and so on, was *The Summing-Up* (1938). 'Once it is finished,' he said, letting the reader in on the excitement of the venture, 'I shall know where I stand.' Partly anecdotal, partly meditative, speculative, dogmatic and philosophical, containing many absorbing thoughts on the problems of story-writing and play-writing, it is a mellow and masterly performance which no one contemplating a career in the world of letters should fail to read.

Desmond MacCarthy thought it was 'a book of exceptional import', and he devoted not just one but two whole lead reviews to it in the second and third week of January 1938 (thereby underlining the advantage review-wise of January publication). This eminent reviewer praised the candour of the self-portrait, the detachment with which Maugham casts himself in an unattractive light during some of the more personal moments, but for him the chief value of the work lies in the examination of Maugham's own artistic conscience, and he takes the opportunity to define, as he sees it, Maugham's relation to the intelligentsia ('highbrows' is MacCarthy's preferred Bloomsbury term). The ambivalence of that relation may be sensed in his analysis of Maugham's career:

Considered as a 'case' Mr Somerset Maugham is remarkable because he was born an intellectual and started as a highbrow writer; [*Liza of Lambeth* – highbrow?] forsook in order to capture success the highbrow's obligation to write 'out for himself', and always to write his best (which is not the same as taking enormous pains to make a decent job of his second best); and then returned in middle life to a deeper sincerity. His career is particularly interesting because he has made the best of both worlds, and with nearly complete awareness of what he was doing. His deviation was, however, not without profit to him as a serious writer. It taught him to avoid certain faults.

The reviewer's embrace is a strange one: somewhere up his sleeve he has a knife which he is prepared to use if only he can get close enough to the victim's back. The stab comes in a spirited defence of Pater, one of Bloomsbury's patron saints:

Mr Maugham hates Pater because he is the prophet of Culture, and Culture he thinks is conceited and out of touch with life. It is a most human and intimate thing. It measures, compares, and remembers more than one single life can teach and contain; that is the essence of it. When Mr Maugham says that it no more profits a man to have read a thousand books than to have ploughed a thousand fields, he is saying a foolish thing, and he is making quite as rash a statement as he does when he says that because 'all men are sinners' – to use the phraseology of the General Confession – there is little to choose between good men and bad.

Two styles of life are at war in this passage: the sedentary bookish life of a top critic who suffers from chronic creative sterility and the outgoing life of an author determined not to become imprisoned by his own innate bookishness. Books were as great a drug for Maugham as they were for MacCarthy but until the end of his life he always resisted total addiction to them.

After the publication of *The Summing-Up* Maugham continued to travel in pursuit of various fictional projects. The early part of 1939 saw him living for a while in a mining community at Lens in Belgium and most impressed by the natural good fellowship of the people. The material he collected was later used in an episode in the career of the hero of *The Razor's Edge*. Maugham also decided at this time to re-visit the British working-class regions of London. He saw his career as a novelist ending as it had begun with a lively portrait of these admirable human beings. He explored Bermondsey and went to the music hall in the company of the Cockney bookseller Fred Bason.

But it was Maugham's meeting around this time with another young man much involved in the compassionate occupation of prison-visiting that was to be the start of a permanent relationship. This was Alan Searle who was to become Maugham's secretary and close companion for the whole of the latter part of his life. His work among London prisoners provided Maugham with ideas for at least two short stories (the tales Maugham describes as told him by Ned Preston). One was the very popular one called 'The Kite' and the other less well known is 'Episode', about an amorous postman who falls out of love with the girl who is waiting for him while he is in prison. Maugham never actually met any of the people who were the originators of this episode yet Mr Searle was astonished by the accuracy with which he depicted them.

Maugham lingered in London throughout the early hot summer of 1939 and he did not arrive back at Cap Ferrat until the middle of July. Robin Maugham accompanied him there as well as Gerald Haxton; his daughter and her husband were due to arrive later and a succession of other visitors throughout the remainder of the summer. Maugham had purchased a yacht, the *Sara*, which was moored in the harbour at Villefranche and registered in Haxton's name and flying the American flag. With the prospect of some pleasant trips in her, pasta cooked on board washed down with *vin rosé*, tennis and swimming in the pool at the Mauresque, convivial company and a long novel about India to brood over, it promised to be a highly typical and extremely agreeable September. In the event the party was to be rudely interrupted.

11

World War Two

Maugham was aboard Gerald Haxton's yacht anchored off Bandol when he heard that war had been declared. They had sailed there from Villefranche on an order from the harbour-master that all private shipping was to leave within twenty-four hours. Bandol was full of craft and they had had some difficulty finding a mooring. A mood of apprehensive camaraderie developed among all the boat-owners as they listened to the radio news and waited for the papers to arrive from Toulon. Next to Bandol was Sanary where Aldous Huxley had once lived, and later the novelist Leon Feuchtwanger, who had escaped there from the Nazis. Now Feuchtwanger had been interned as an enemy alien. Maugham intervened on his behalf with the French writer Jean Giraudoux whom he knew slightly. Giraudoux was head of the Bureau of Information in Paris. Eventually Feuchtwanger was released.

After a period of enforced leisure on the *Sara*, Maugham and Gerald decided to return to the Mauresque before they died of bore-dom. Not only was it empty now of guests but several of the staff, especially those who were Italian, had left too. Meanwhile the navy and the military had moved into the region. There was a camp on the road below, anti-aircraft guns had been installed on the cliff, and on the top of a hill that was part of Maugham's property, was a signals unit.

Under these conditions Maugham did not feel able to continue his creative work. He was glad of a chore which had been wished on him by his publishers, to edit a collection of aphorisms and witty sayings from his own work. He was gradually becoming as much in demand, particularly in the United States, as a commentator upon literature as he was as a writer of it. People enjoyed reading the classic works that he recommended. A mammoth editorial task which he had recently undertaken was an anthology of a hundred outstanding short stories from England, France, Russia and Germany, with a long introduction tracing the history of the form and discussing the work of its greatest exponents. Doubleday published this collection in 1939 in America as *Tellers of Tales* (later *The Greatest Stories of All Times*) but the war seems to have killed off the British publication. This was a pity because Maugham's choices are fascinating, not so much for their unpredictable nature as for their catholicity as a whole. He by no means sticks to his own type of story.

Kipling's 'Without Benefit of Clergy' is there, so is Stephen Crane's 'An Experiment in Misery', H.G. Wells's 'The Door in the Wall', Max Beerbohm's 'A.V. Laider', D.H. Lawrence's 'Odour of Chrysanthemums', Katherine Mansfield's 'The Stranger', Katherine Anne Porter's 'María Concepcíon', Dorothy Parker's 'Big Blonde' and Isherwood's 'The Nowaks' – to name but a few. Much of the substance of the introduction appeared in a later essay on 'The Short Story' in *Points of View*. From now on Maugham felt with justice that this was a subject on which he had the right to pronounce. He gave a lecture on it to the Royal Society of Literature in 1947.

Among the mail that had piled up at the Mauresque while they had been away was a letter from the British authorities in London thanking Maugham for the offer of his services to help in the war effort (he had written off immediately) and telling him to stand by. He expected to be summoned back to England, but when his instructions did arrive, after considerable delay, they contained a request for him to write a series of articles on France and the war. He went to Paris for a briefing, saw Giraudoux and others, before setting off on his travels around France. The *entente* was not very *cordiale* at the time and Maugham's job was to write something that would make it more real. He was shown a part of the Maginot line; he went into munitions factories and down in a submarine; army headquarters and refugee centres were thrown open for his inspection. Many of the officials he saw had heard of him and knew something of his work. They welcomed the *Maître* with open arms. He for his part wrote several articles of glowing optimism about the state of morale in France and the confidence he had in the ability of the French to fight the war successfully. These appeared in magazines in Britain, they were then collected and published as a sixpenny pamphlet in 1940 entitled *France at War* which to Maugham's amazement (and later considerable embarrassment) sold 100,000 copies. Publication was discontinued after the fall of

France. Then Maugham told the full story of his experiences, the venality and the cynicism he had also observed in France during the early days of the war, in *Strictly Personal*.

After he had completed his articles Maugham boarded an aircraft for the first time in his life, incredible as it sounds, to find out in London what his next assignment was. He met several of Neville Chamberlain's ministers but no one could think of how best to employ him. He compared himself at this time to 'a performing dog in a circus whose tricks the public would probably like, but who somehow couldn't be quite fitted into the programme'. His thoughts became focused on the United States. Eventually someone in the Ministry of Information suggested he should write a series of articles about Britain to match those he had done on France. According to Maugham this was not nearly so easy. In England an author was a writing feller to be kept strictly in his place and not to be given the *entrée* anywhere important. Before the project really got off the ground, however, the Germans invaded Norway and it was felt Maugham would be much better occupied back in France. On his return he found Gerald in the Mauresque keeping things going; somehow he had obtained permission to take the *Sara* back to her berth at Villefranche.

Even after Dunkirk they stayed on. Like everyone else in France they believed that the French army's withdrawal was part of a deliberate plan. They confidently expected Weygand to make a stand. Suddenly Paul Reynaud resigned and Pétain took over, signalling that the end had come. Maugham went to his gardener's cottage and saw the man and his wife weeping with shame. Maugham wept with them. Afterwards he went into Nice where with a crowd of other British expatriates he heard that they were being advised to leave France and that two colliery vessels were lying off Cannes to take them out. He had to be there with a blanket and three days' provisions by eight the next morning.

Ever since Borneo he had had a fear of death by drowning, but after some soul-searching he decided to risk the voyage. Haxton, as a citizen of what was then still a neutral country, stayed on to close down the villa and to try to store its art treasures and other valuables for the duration. What, though, of Maugham's work in progress? There was the typescript of the anthology of his work, bulky but not irreplaceable; his notes on the Indian trip and a selection in two volumes of typescript from all the Notebooks he had kept since he was a medical student of eighteen. Gerald said he

H. Andrew Freeth's etching of
Somerset Maugham.

would take these and the Indian notes down to the *Sara* – as she
flew the American flag they fondly imagined she would be un-
molested in the event of an invasion. A few pages back we saw Desmond MacCarthy berating Maugham for putting practical skills
above culture in the scheme of things. Yet now at this moment of
crisis Maugham behaved like a confirmed man of culture. He
lumbered his grip with three books, *The Trial and Death of Socrates*,
Esmond and *Villette*, the first seemed appropriate, the others were
long novels he had not read for some time. He did not pack any
towels or soap but he did put in a dinner jacket.

Thirteen hundred Britons stood on the quay at Cannes waiting
to embark in the two coal ships. Along with five hundred other
people Maugham boarded one called the *Saltersgate*. Conditions on
board were appalling. The vessel had lavatory accommodation for
a crew of thirty-eight. They were told they were making for Oran
in Algeria to await instructions from Gibraltar. When they arrived
there news of the capitulation of France had come through and they
were sent on to Gibraltar with only an hour or so for shopping.
Even when they arrived at Gibraltar only the old and the infirm
were permitted to land. Maugham and the rest then had to endure

a nightmare journey back to England of which he gave later a memorable account in *Strictly Personal.*

Maugham stayed at the Dorchester as was his usual practice when in London. In spite of air raids and sandbags some guests were still dressing for dinner and trying to carry on as if nothing had hit them. But when Maugham went out and about he observed a change of mood. His friend Winston Churchill who had taken over from Chamberlain as Prime Minister was entering into his era of glory. In spite of the nation's isolation and difficulties there was a new optimistic spirit of total commitment to the war. Maugham had meetings with some of Churchill's closest colleagues. He saw A.V. Alexander, First Lord of the Admiralty, and Sir Alan Brooke (later Lord Alanbroke) who assured him of his confidence in the morale of the troops and of the civilian population. He also met an old friend from the Riviera, Lord Beaverbrook, now Minister for Aircraft Production, and Ernest Bevin, Minister of Labour, whose buoyant manner greatly impressed him. Maugham was given access to factories and he was fascinated to observe the entertainment provided in the canteen during the lunch break. He prophesied the Labour victory after the war and he saw that there would have to be a redistribution of wealth. He felt, too, that true national unity could only come when all children had the same educational opportunities. The Headmaster of his old school at Canterbury, Canon Shirley, had written to Maugham suggesting a rapprochement, but this did not come to anything until after the war.

The result of his various high-level meetings was inconclusive. They felt and he felt that his propagandist role, his talents as a cultural mediator, could be most profitably pursued in the United States where he had many friends and a vast public. Moreover at this time United States opinion was not by any means unanimously on the side of Britain. If anyone could bridge the emotional and intellectual gulf that separated the two English-speaking nations that person, it seemed, was Maugham. He was given a nebulous brief to write something that would put the plight of Britain and the courage of the British people vividly before American readers. He left London and after a tedious delay of several weeks in Lisbon he arrived at La Guardia airport in New York in October 1940, where he was met by Nelson and Ellen Doubleday. Maugham's first gesture was to order a bourbon old fashioned at the bar in the airport. According to Garson Kanin, 'He drank it with great relish and thanked the Doubledays. Whereupon he took an ampoule of poison out of his vest pocket, put it on the floor, and crushed it under his heel, saying, "I won't need this now, Nelson." '

The British Treasury agreed to let Maugham have $2,500 a month of his dollar assets and Doubleday, his American publishers, were only too happy to advance him further sums on his earnings. His war-time exile promised to be fairly comfortable which for an eminent man already over retiring age but with a job of work to do was reasonable. He took a suite of three rooms at the Ritz-Carlton while awaiting somewhere more permanent. The Doubledays were plan-ning to build a house for him on their estate at Yemassee in South Carolina. Meanwhile Haxton had got out of France and had for the moment joined Maugham at the Ritz. Maugham's daughter Liza was in New York too.

There were a number of British writers attached to the American division of the Ministry of Information at this time, among them novelist Cecil Roberts who became a friend of Maugham's. He captured the febrile mood of New York 1940 in the volume of his autobiography called *Sunshine and Shadow* (1972). Harley Granville Barker was another exile. He had played the hero in the very first production of Maugham's very first play *A Man of Honour* way back in 1903 when they had not got on at all well. In *The Summing-Up* Maugham had described him as 'a young man brimming over with other people's ideas'; now, forty years on, they became friendly. Yet another eminent English writer, spreading his own particular gospel in New York, was H.G. Wells. Somehow though the fizz had gone out of him. He gave a series of lectures which were a dis-aster. 'People couldn't hear what he said,' Maugham noted, not, one feels, without a certain malicious pleasure, 'and didn't want to listen to what they could hear. They left in droves. He was hurt and disappointed.'

Maugham's shuttling between France, England, Portugal and the United States had not in any way lessened his output of published work. On the contrary the hazards of the time only seemed to stimu-late him to ever more intensive literary effort. *Books and You*, the first of his volumes of literary *causerie*, had appeared in March, and now he began to recall the saga of his flight from France for *Redbook* magazine before it was published in book form as *Strictly Personal*. He also wrote a short novel set in Florence, *Up at the Villa*, whose only indication of the period is the presence of refugees roaming around and prompting the heroine, fatally, to keep a loaded revolver in her bedroom. Maugham wrote it mainly to boost his American bank account. He was also mindful of his propaganda mission, and wrote a number of magazine articles trying to explain the subtleties of the British temperament to Americans and vice versa. One of these pieces called 'Why Do You Dislike Us?', which was published in *The Saturday Evening Post* in April 1942, provoked 7,000 angry readers to write letters answering Maugham's query in no uncertain terms. A gentleman named Kelly asked, 'Do you think we shall ever forget the battle of the Boyne?' These wartime articles remain uncollected among his published works. Hard to come by, too, is his other major piece of propaganda, the novel *The Hour Before The Dawn* which was published in the United States by Doubleday in 1942, after serialization in *Redbook*, but never published in Britain. It tells rather woodenly the story of the impact of the war upon a typical English family and their neighbours in the country; in it is evidence of Maugham's obsession with the possibility of refugees from Nazi Germany containing a fifth column. It was a book Maugham later rather regretted ever having written as he explained in a letter to his friend Eddie Marsh to whom he normally submitted all his work before publication for meticulous proof-reading and final grammatical correction: 'I knew very well it was poor and I was miserable about it. I tried to console myself by looking upon it as my contribution to the war effort, but that did not help much and I prefer to think now that it will be unread in England and forgotten in America...?' Time would appear to have granted him his wish.

From the Ritz Maugham went west with Haxton to California and Hollywood where in 1941 for a while he rented a house in Beverly Glen. Garson Kanin's wife, the actress Ruth Gordon, was making a movie at the time and she arranged a dinner party for Maugham at the house of the French director, René Clair. In spite of the exquisite food and wine it was a disaster because the star guest and the host, Maugham and Clair, took an instant dislike to each other. Maugham was in fact going through a profoundly anti-French phase at this time as is clear from his writings. He refused requests to contribute to the Free French magazines that had begun to appear because he disapproved of their printing soothing articles to France's wounded spirit by foreign writers whereas he felt that, 'for years now she has been a second-class power masquerading as a first-class one... The war has made manifest what only the very astute saw.' Maugham's ambivalent attitude towards France to which he would none the less return as soon as the war was over is also reflected in a short story he wrote called 'The Unconquered', which appeared first in *Colliers' Magazine* in April 1943. A young French girl is made pregnant by a German soldier who afterwards offers to marry her and to run her parents' farm when her brother is killed. The old farmer and his wife are won over by the German and are all for collaboration: the girl however resists their pressure and drowns her baby as soon as it is born. It is a harsh story with its moral melodramatically stated but a remarkable feat of the imagination in that Maugham was remote from France when he wrote it.

Maugham was not the only renowned British author in exile in Southern California at this time. Aldous Huxley, Christoper Isher-

A scene from the film of *A Razor's Edge*, *from left to right* Gene Tierney, Clifton Webb, Herbert Marshall, Anne Baxter, John Payne and Tyrone Power.

wood and Gerald Heard had all been living there for some time
and had all been engaged in the study of Vedanta and the practice
of meditation. Thus for a while Maugham's pattern of interests and
theirs coincided; critics have seen a kinship between the work they
produced during this period, between for instance *The Razor's Edge*
and *Time Must Have a Stop*, both published in 1944. Obviously
there is some kinship: all four men were highly accurate antennae
of a movement that was just beginning to sweep across the west
and exert a profound influence upon our culture. But there is an
important difference between Maugham and the Anglo-Californian
vedantaists: they were primarily believers and he was an observer.
They were converts whereas Maugham for all his interest and
admiration remained sceptical. They were actually getting up in the
small hours and meditating and going to the Vedanta centre in
Hollywood and sitting at the feet of Swami Prabhavananda, a Hindu
monk of the Ramakrishna Order, whereas Maugham was checking
through his notes on the Maharishi, rescued by Gerald, in preparation for his next book. Compare the level of empathy with and
understanding of Vedanta in *The Razor's Edge* and in Isherwood's
Meeting by the River, and you see the difference.

At Yemassee, thanks to the kindness of the Doubledays, a bungalow had been built to accommodate Maugham. He had a separate
writing-shack to which he could escape in total isolation from his
servants, a gardener, cook and maid, of whom he became extremely
fond and taught to serve an exotic dinner party menu for occasional
visitors. Maugham moved in there for the duration and soon established his regular routine of writing. Gerald went to Washington
DC where he was employed by the Government of the United States
which since the bombardment of Pearl Harbor by the Japanese in
1941 was now no longer neutral.

With the war now in a new phase the British Information authorities in the United States did not feel any pressing urgency to employ
Maugham as a propagandist, and he was left more and more to his
own devices. This suited him admirably. He had a huge amount
of work he wanted to do and he was more than happy to live the
life of a literary recluse at Parker's Ferry as his place was called.
One cause for anxiety was Gerald's health which was bad, another
was money which he seems to have worried about unduly at this
period. By ordinary standards he certainly had enough. He even
used to go for little working holidays in the summer to Edgartown
on Martha's Vineyard Island and stay in a hotel. As an economy

measure he restricted himself to one room but the management insisted he had a sitting-room at no extra charge.

But with petrol rationing now in force even Maugham's passion for travel had to be curbed and for the most part he was content to stay at home and see no one, apart from the coloured servants. He loved to wander in the woods at the back of his bungalow and to listen to the susurrus of the wind in the trees as he meditated upon the differences between the English and the American character, or upon the ultimate purpose and significance of life. In his book he was tracing the character of a young man who appears to opt out of life – long before that became commonplace – to renounce the competitive struggle for wealth and material success and devote himself to contemplation and understanding. Maugham had used this idea to structure a plot several times before in both stories and plays, and he referred to two previous works especially in mapping out his new book. One was a story going back almost to the days of 'Rain', called 'The Fall of Edward Barnard', in which a young man seduced by the pleasures of the South Seas where he has a job sacrifices his marriage to the daughter of a Chicago tycoon, and the other is a play with a variant of the same plot called *The Road Uphill*. It appears to have been written in 1924 but was never actually performed. A copy of the script which has not been published was discovered by Raymond Mander and Joe Mitchenson when they were working on their *Theatrical Companion to the Plays of Maugham* where it is summarized. They kindly lent me the text.

Certainly the parallels with *The Razor's Edge* are striking. Here we have the same trio of young people in Chicago with both the men in love with the girl; the sympathetic one whom she loves does not want to work in business, instead he wants to be a painter, an ambition that fails him (like the young man in 'Alien Corn'). Then he withdraws totally from life whereas the unsympathetic one joins the corporation, becomes rich, and marries her. The play shuttles from Chicago to Paris and back over about five years. In the end the sympathetic young man writes what promises to be an outstanding work of philosophy (like Eilert Lovborg) so all ends happily.

But what most people remember about *The Razor's Edge* is not so much the mysticism, or even the central figure, sympathetic though he is, but the surrounding characters, especially the social-climbing art-peddling Elliot Templeton, and the sweeping view it contains of pre-war society in Chicago, Paris and on the French Riviera, and above all the personality of the narrator, the urbane and worldly novelist who while surprised by nothing himself springs so many delectable surprises upon us. All this was inserted into the original scheme of the plot over two years of intensive work at Parker's Ferry in some of Maugham's mellowest and most readable prose.

The Razor's Edge was published in 1944, first of all in April in the United States, and then in July in Britain. Diana Trilling reviewing it in the *Nation* commented that, 'Mysticism... is bound to be inviting to the person who is afraid of the deep emotions; yet it can never fully win him. All the characters in Maugham's latest novel inevitably inhabit the non-dimensional universe which is all that is left when the deep emotions have been disavowed.' Many of the other reviewers agreed that Larry inhabited a non-dimensional universe but they were delighted, as I am still, by the rest of the book. Cyril Connolly was, for example, warm in praise of the book in a review in the *New Statesman and Nation* entitled 'The Art of Being Good' in which he described it as Maugham's best novel since *Cakes and Ale* and 'powerful propaganda for the new faith'. The public on both sides of the Atlantic endorsed the Connolly rather than the Trilling verdict as they went to the bookstores to obtain the novel. The book's British publisher A.S. Frere, remembers its reception:

People were looking and reaching out for something which Willie in this book calls goodness and all the rest of it. And of course if he'd really cynically set out to write the immediate post-war best-seller he couldn't have hit a more likely subject. The book after all sold seven million copies in hard-cover. I remember around this time Lord Maugham, that's Willie's brother Freddie, was giving me lunch and Evelyn Waugh (who was not unpleased to be lunching in the House of Lords) was at the next table talking in a loud voice and saying he'd just published a book [*Brideshead Revisited*] which he said was a bestseller in America and over here. Viscount Maugham overheard this and turned to him and said, 'Young man, you say you're a bestseller! I have a brother whose just written a book which has sold seven million copies.'

Since the book was published there has been endless speculation about the originals of some of the characters. Christopher Isherwood has often been put forward as the model for Larry, but as we have seen Larry was already fully fledged as Joe in *The Road Uphill* when Isherwood was only four years old. If there was a model it seems to have been an obscure young man whom Maugham met for about twenty minutes when he was driving him across New York

Maugham with his brother, the Lord Chancellor: a considerable coolness developed between the two in adult life.

OPPOSITE
Graham Sutherland's portrait of A.S. Frere, Maugham's British publisher.

in a taxi thus suggesting Larry's end. Then again there are several candidates for the real Elliot Templeton. Garson Kanin takes quite seriously the idea that it was Henry James. How would the Master have reacted to that? 'The all flattering and beautifully concealed identification is, as it were, ever so finely "wide of the mark".' Another strongly supported candidate is the Duke of Windsor's friend 'Chips' Channon who actually claimed the honour after the book appeared. But no, he will not do either. The real Elliot Templeton is a Riviera character well known to Maugham, one Henry May. What does it matter? The invented character will be remembered long after the real one has been forgotten.

Maugham's triumph over the sales of *The Razor's Edge* was spoiled by growing anxiety about Haxton. He had developed pleurisy while in Washington after which tuberculosis had set in. Maugham who had seen the one other human being on this earth he truly loved die of that disease took him to a sanatorium in the Adirondack Mountains. But the treatment did not arrest the disease. Gerald Haxton died in November aged fifty-two in the Doctors' Hospital, New York. Maugham was completely shattered, Cecil Roberts rang him to offer his condolence and asked to come to see him:

'I don't want to see you! I don't want to see anyone! I want to die!' he cried in a distressed voice, and put down the telephone. Nevertheless, I went along to the Ritz and up to his room. He opened the door, very haggard in appearance. I walked in and talked to him firmly. It was noon. He said, 'Let's go down and lunch.' We lunched in the little Japanese garden beside the artificial running stream. When I left he was in a normal mood. 'You are a good friend, Cecil,' he said, holding both my hands. Later, he went down to his Carolina retreat, where his nephew, Robin, joined him.

When Maugham finally got around to publishing his carefully censored and edited selections from his fifteen volumes of Notebooks (what superb material must have perished in the remainder he destroyed) *A Writer's Notebook* in 1949, perhaps the richest of all his works, he thought of the man who had shared with him many of the experiences described therein. Thus the dedication reads: 'In Loving Memory of My Friend Frederick Gerald Haxton 1892–1944.'

One of the most memorable passages in this book is that under the year 1944 which describes how Maugham felt on reaching the age of seventy. He spent his birthday alone, apart from the servants, at Parker's Ferry. He worked as usual in the morning, went for a walk in the woods after lunch, made a cup of tea, read till dinnertime. After dinner he read again, played some games of patience, listened to the news, took a detective story to bed, finished it and went to sleep. A typical Maugham day. At seventy, he reckoned, one was no longer on the threshold of old age. One was just an old man. Maugham was always eager to assume the role appropriate to his years. From now on he refers to himself as The Old Party.

As soon as *The Razor's Edge* was in typescript, copies had been circulated in Hollywood. It was bought for filming by Daryl F. Zanuck who commissioned a script from Lamar Trotti. George Cukor saw it and did not like it. He said to Zanuck he would do the picture if he could get Maugham to do the script. Zanuck replied Maugham would be too expensive. Then, as Gavin Lambert shows in his con-

George Cukor who directed *The Razor's Edge*.

versations with the director in *On Cukor*, Cukor phoned Maugham who said he would do the script for nothing. Maugham came out to Hollywood and stayed with Cukor while writing a script which the director liked very much. It began with some advice to the players:

Please note that this is, on the whole, a comedy and should be played lightly by everyone except in the definitely serious passages. The actors should pick up one another's cues as smartly as possible, and there's no harm if they cut in on one another as people do in ordinary life. I'm all against pauses and silences. If the actors cannot give significance to their lines without these they're not worth their salaries. The lines are written to be spoken; they have all the significance needed if they are spoken with intelligence and feeling. The director is respectfully reminded that

Maugham dining at the Villa
Mauresque with Alan Searle who
became his secretary after the Second
World War.

the action should accompany and illustrate the dialogue. Speed, speed,
speed.

It seemed to be all set up but such is the way of Hollywood that
in the end Cukor did not direct the picture and the script by Trotti
was used in preference to Maugham's. Instead of payment the
studio bought Maugham a painting. This came down to a choice
between a snow scene by Matisse or a picture of the harbour at
Rouen by Pissarro. He chose the Matisse but later exchanged it for
the Pissarro.

Before Maugham left the United States at the end of the war to
return to the Villa Mauresque he wished to show some token of
the gratitude he felt for the hospitality which he and his daughter
and her family had received there during this troubled period.
Accordingly he presented the manuscript of *Of Human Bondage*
to the Library of Congress in April 1946, and gave an address in
the Coolidge Auditorium explaining how the novel came to be
written, with a digression on the art of fiction. Four years later he
followed this by presenting the unpublished manuscript of the
novel's earlier incarnation 'The Artistic Temperament of Stephen
Carey' to the Library.

On returning to France he found his villa ravaged externally by
shell-fire and internally by military occupation, but his art collection
was safe. Maugham and his new secretary and companion, Alan
Searle, set about the formidable task of restoring the Mauresque to
its former glory.

12

Vagrant Moods

The last twenty years of Maugham's life were full of strange contradictions. He was never more successful yet never more embittered. He spent much time mentally preparing for death yet his attachment to life was tenacious. When he was seventy walking in the woods of the Yemassee he doubted whether he would write any more novels, yet of three for which he had ideas he completed two. The third about Bermondsey life was to have brought his career as a novelist to a close, as it had begun fifty years earlier with a study of the London poor. However, he scrapped it when, on revisiting the borough after the war, he discovered that it had changed out of all recognition. He was at his happiest now, at his most creative that is, when he was thinking back over his own life or recreating the lives of people in the recent or remote past (like Augustus Hare, the Victorian traveller) whom he admired or had known. He had one more volume of short stories to give the world, *Creatures of Circumstance* in 1947, a round-up of tales written over a wide span of time, and containing such gems as 'The Colonel's Lady'. He told Garson Kanin he had found the idea for this on the back of an envelope while staying at the Ritz in New York and had dashed it off before leaving. 'It paid for my stay,' he said, 'which was expensive.'

In general his outlook now was retrospective. He had lived through a great many different periods from the Victorian to the contemporary and through his wanderings among the great monuments of western civilization he had inhabited in his imagination a great many more. He became a vagrant among his memories; to revive them he would travel in countries he had visited when he was younger, revisiting with Alan places he had been to originally with Gerald. Only this time he was a world-famous celebrity and his arrival would be marked by the presence of film and television cameras, and become an occasion for civic receptions. The novelist

and critic Francis King, who was Director of the British Council in Kyoto after the war, remembers the excitement caused by Maugham's arrival in Japan, the event being blazoned across the front pages of newspapers:

When we were going round the temple students would rush up having recognized him in the newspapers and say 'Mr Maugham, Mr Maugham please sign this for me,' and ask him for his autograph. Wherever one went, any garden, any temple, people would come up as if to touch the hem of his garment. I think he really enjoyed it. This kind of thing must have been very gratifying for him, to be treated as a really great writer.

The one place where he was not so treated, he noted, was in London. There all he got when he arrived for his annual summer sojourn at the Dorchester was a few lines in the Londoner's Diary in *The Evening Standard*. Yet even in his native land he was not entirely without honour. He was made a Companion of Honour by the Queen, a Doctor of Literature by Oxford, and a Fellow of the Royal Society of Literature. In the popular mind Maugham became a success-symbol. For a time his presence had something of the aura that would later surround the pop stars. This came about largely through the films that were made out of his short stories in *Quartet* (1948), *Trio* (1950) and *Encore* (1952). Sydney Box, the producer, had the brilliant idea of giving a unity to the separate stories of which each film was composed by making Maugham himself appear on the terrace of the Mauresque on a beautiful summer's day, and introduce each screenplay with a few moments of stammering, disarming chat. Maugham as the urbane narrator, who can't at this distance of time remember how much is fact and how much is fiction, gave the most immaculate performance. He imposed himself on the audience as a living embodiment of the pains and rewards of literature as a profession.

Other institutions, their gaze less fixated on the box office, were quick none the less to recognize Maugham's prowess as a performer, and his services were much in demand. He gave a masterly lecture to the Kipling Society in the presence of Kipling's daughter, explaining why he regarded him as the greatest English writer of short stories. This afterwards became the basis for the introduction to his *A Choice of Kipling's Prose* (1952). He spoke in New York to the Philosophical Colloquium of the University of Columbia and, in London, to the National Book League on 'The Writer's Point of View,' affirming his belief that by following the calling of

ABOVE
Sir Gerald Kelly at work on one of his portraits of Maugham.

OPPOSITE
Nigel Patrick as Max Kelada in 'Mr Knowall', one of three Maugham stories that formed the film *Trio*.

an author a person, whether he succeed or fail, 'will lead a life of inexhaustible interest and enjoy, as few can in this world of today, the inestimable pleasure of freedom'.

The most sparkling of Maugham's post-war public utterances was the speech he made at the Royal Academy dinner in 1951. His old friend Gerald Kelly had been elected President of the Academy in 1949. Like Maugham he too had reached his seventieth birthday. 'Do you remember Paris in 1904?' asked Maugham in the course of his prompt letter of congratulation. 'We did not imagine then that either of us would come to the point we have' ... And he added: 'Finally, I hope you will be as urbane and tolerant of other people's stupidity in your new position as your irascible temper will permit. After all you have to make up for your predecessor's [Sir Alfred

Munnings's] mistakes if you want to maintain the dignity of the institution.'

In his outspoken way Kelly maintained the dignity of the Institution extremely well, not least at the annual dinner. It is a formidable occasion at which to have to make a speech, and in those days it used to be broadcast live to the nation by the BBC. The speakers in 1951 were Clement Attlee, the then Prime Minister; Winston Churchill who was enjoying a rest from government, Maugham would see him on the Riviera, a paintbrush or a cigar in hand; Admiral Lord Cork and Orrery; Lord Samuel and Somerset Maugham. It was the last-named who stole the show when he proposed the toast to literature.

Maugham left nothing to chance. In order to produce the effect he wanted for the ten minutes or so he was on his feet he put as much effort into it as into one of his stories. He began with an anecdote of a tweedy lady from Cheltenham he pretended he had encountered in the Academy during the annual summer exhibition and Sherlock Holmes-like he inferred her entire life-history (her Anglo-Indian father who served in the army in Poona, the various subalterns to whom she was engaged) from a glance at her clothes. Finally, after getting a laugh for each additional telling stroke to the portrait, Maugham played his ace. 'And then I knew who she was: she was the lady who doesn't know much about art but knows what she likes' – and this led Maugham to wind up with some unexceptional remarks about picture-buying and the vagaries of fashion in art.

Kelly's biographer, Derek Hudson, says that over the years Kelly painted some eighteen portraits of Maugham from the obscure struggling author of 1907 to the very old party of 1963. No less than fifteen of these are in the Humanities Research Center of the University of Texas. Nor was he the only one by any means. Maugham was a subject no portraitist could resist. One of the most revealing portraits is by the French artist with a Scottish name, Edouard MacAvoy who gets the set of the head and the torso remarkably well in a cubistic arrangement of Maugham's muscular frame. And then there are those by Marie Laurencin with soft pinks and yellows that are not really like him but capture the romanticism beneath the cynic's mask.

However, the portrait that we all remember and which made incarnate the myth of Maugham, as the Chinese sorcerer wrapt in his mystical aloofness, is that by Graham Sutherland. The artist was

staying at St Jean Cap Ferrat in the spring of 1948; a friend of his, Eardley Knollys, took him to lunch with Maugham. Sutherland explains what happened next.

On the way home I said to Mr Knollys, if I were a portrait painter, that is the kind of face I might make something of. He repeated this to Monroe Wheeler of the Museum of Modern Art in New York (a friend of Maugham's). Maugham then asked me to paint his portrait. At first I refused, feeling it was an undertaking too complicated for one who was not a professional portrait painter. Finally he persuaded me and I agreed on condition that the matter be considered as an experiment with no obligation on either side.

Maugham and Sutherland being
interviewed together on television.

Maugham claimed to be very pleased with the result. He could
hardly do otherwise in the circumstances. As for Sutherland this
portrait marked, as Douglas Cooper says in his *Sutherland* (1961),
an important turning-point: 'A new vein of inspiration opened up
for Sutherland when he began to see in the lines, forms and convolu-
tions of the human face the same sort of expression of the process
of growth and struggle as he found in the rugged surfaces and
irregular contours of a boulder or a range of hills.' It led to further
portraits, several of the subjects being men of power and influence
who were in the orbit of Maugham, like Churchill, Beaverbrook
and A.S. Frere.

The Riviera had once again become Maugham's permanent
home, and in spite of his harsh words about the French he became a
Companion of the Legion d'Honneur, a distinction he found very
useful when travelling in France as he explained to Kelly when the
artist was awarded the same decoration. But in his old age
Maugham was mindful of his English, indeed his Kentish roots.
Even before the war he had privately returned to Canterbury,
to mooch about the precincts and cloisters, and had formed a wish
to be laid to rest beside the Cathedral when he died. Canon F.J. Shirley, who was both a great headmaster and a great fund-raiser, had
suggested at that time that he write a play to be performed for the
benefit of the school. He had immediately rejected that idea, but
he did now accept an invitation to sit alongside the Dean and
Chapter of Canterbury on the Governing Body of The King's
School. He was punctilious about attending meetings when he was
in England and on one occasion in 1948 he spent two days at the
school enjoying a fireside chat with some of the boys. He remembered the crushing class-consciousness, the stifling élitism of his own
schooldays and he suggested to Shirley that he should donate the
money for a fund to,

provide education in a public school for the sons of working men, and
the motive for its institution was to diminish the class-consciousness of
the ordinary schoolboy by throwing him into contact at a formative period
of his life with boys of another class, and thus to some extent to diminish
the exclusiveness and snobbery which have resulted in the universal dislike for the English which no traveller abroad can fail to notice. The Duke
of Wellington is supposed to have said that the Battle of Waterloo was
won on the playing fields of Eton. I think a future historian may with
more truth say that India was lost in the public schools of England.

That Maugham continued to feel very strongly about this is clear

The pictures on these and the following pages were taken at the Villa Mauresque. Maugham's lifestyle there was affluent, hospitable and industrious.

from the foreword he wrote in 1954 to the memoirs of his friend Aga Khan where we find similar sentiments expressed. But even Maugham's munificence could only provide a scholarship for one boy to attend The King's School and the scheme never really got off the ground, bravely ahead of its time as it was. Instead Maugham became a benefactor in other ways. He may well have been spurred on in his generosity by the fact Hugh Walpole, another alumnus, had made some notable bequests. At any rate Maugham provided the money for Chippendale furniture and eighteenth-century mezzotints for the Masters' Common Room, a new science block, new boathouses and rowing equipment, and above all the Maugham Library to which he left a section of his own library, including many first editions of his own works and the manuscripts of his first and last novels, *Liza of Lambeth* and *Catalina*. (In common with other students of Maugham the present writer has enjoyed visiting the library and browsing among its treasures.)

Catalina appeared in 1948. It concerned the miraculous vision of a young peasant girl in sixteenth-century Spain and traced amusingly all the ramifying high-level intrigue in church and state set in train by the event. It was one of the two playfully conceived period novels Maugham had set himself to write before he retired. The other one, even more satirical in spirit, seized upon a moment in the career of Niccolò Macchiavelli when he was involved on behalf of the city of Florence in a delicate negotiation with the powerful and dangerous Caesar Borgia, at the same time trying to bed the young wife of a friend. Maugham's somewhat too ingenious notion is to show the real events, both momentous and ludicrous, that led Macchiavelli to write *The Prince* and his play *Mandragola*. The historical situation is complex even for so normally lucid an expositor and it takes some time of rather ponderous prose before the narrative comes to life, allowing Maugham to enjoy his fun with diplomatic and amorous games of bluff and double-bluff at the heart of the book.

Edmund Wilson, the American critic who led the attack on Maugham's reputation.

Unfortunately, coming as it did in the wake of *The Razor's Edge*, this very slight work, *Then and Now*, raised the highest expectations. It was published more or less simultaneously on both sides of the Atlantic in May; Doubleday and Heinemann each printed an edition of 50,000 copies, a massive first edition even for Maugham. The detractors were lying in wait for him. Edmund Wilson who was then reviewing books regularly in *The New Yorker* used the clumsiness apparent in parts of the novel as the preliminary to a murderous attack on Maugham's entire reputation as an author. Wilson opened his onslaught with this sentence: 'It has happened to me from time to time to run into some person of taste who tells me I ought to take Somerset Maugham seriously, yet I have never been able to convince myself he was anything but second-rate.' He then went on to quote some rather dire chunks of the background exposition in support of his observation that, 'The language is such a tissue of clichés that one's wonder is finally aroused at the writer's ability to assemble so many and at his unfailing inability to put anything in an individual way.'

It is rather as if a man were dismissing Shakespeare out of hand on the strength of some of the weaker scenes in *Pericles*. But then Wilson broadens his attack to include Maugham's literary judgements on Joyce and Proust in his anthologies and his speech to the Library of Congress. He particularly objects to Maugham's view of Proust as essentially a comic writer and to the comment that, 'We skip his philosophical disquisitions and we skip them without loss.' Maugham, says Wilson, looks up at the great peaks and eminences of modern literature with 'a malcontent eye ... There is something going on, on the higher ground, that halfway compels his respect, but he does not quite understand what it is, and in any case he can never get up there.'

Well, there is clearly a case to answer. Francis King was quoted just now as saying that it must have been gratifying for Maugham when he went to Japan to be treated as a really great writer. The implication is that it was especially gratifying to him because he was not one. I think we would all agree that he was certainly not great in the sense that Henry James and Proust and Tolstoy are. Maugham does occupy the middle ground. He occupies it more brilliantly perhaps than it has even been occupied before. But then does one always wish to be living on the heights? The higher up you go the further away you get from the common universal concerns of men and women. Maugham understood how to dramatize those concerns in such a way as to be readily comprehended by many people not normally attracted by literature, as well as those who are.

In his latter years Maugham had what seems to me the laudable object of wanting to share with his vast public the pleasure he had found all his life in the work of many of the greatest English, French and American writers, the Spanish painters and one or two German philosophers. He insisted that the whole venture should only be undertaken in a spirit of pleasure and he was prepared to recommend the barbarous practice of skipping if there were any danger of boredom descending to stifle enjoyment, though I doubt if he ever skipped anything himself. In general the essays collected in his last books, *The Vagrant Mood* (1952), *Ten Novels and their Authors* (1954) and *Points of View* (1959) seem to me to be models of mediation, full of observations and insights which send the reader rushing back to their subjects with renewed zest and savour.

If only they had been the last things he wrote and published and he had passed out of life in the state of serene, thankful contentment he seems to have found under the shadow of war in the woods at Yemassee. But Maugham played Lear, as it were, the wrong way round. He did the storm scene at the end. If at seventy he had been absolute for death, secure in his comprehension of the Vedanta, desirous of releasing himself from the bondage of terrestrial existence – at eighty he had become more attached than ever, eager

OPPOSITE
Maugham with his nephew and fellow
novelist, Robin, in 1965.

to remain indefinitely on the platform, never to board the train, staying permanently among those who had come to see him off and
enjoying their evident discomfort. In 1954 he and Alan Searle went
to Dr Niehans' clinic and they *both* took the rejuvenation treatment
in common with those other eminent long-lifers, General de Gaulle
and Charlie Chaplin.

All seemed well for a while. Life at the Mauresque went on as
smoothly and as splendidly as ever. There were rumours of a book
of memoirs. But gradually there were increasing signs of peevish-
ness and tension. Maugham became inordinately possessive. He
could not bear to let Alan out of his sight for a second. The life
of his devoted secretary became positively hellish. Frere went to
lunch at the Mauresque and found Maugham in a terrible state
imagining people would leap out from the shadows and knife him in
the back. It was clear to him that Maugham was going out of his
mind. In his semi-lucid moments Maugham appears to have real-
ized what was happening and to have feared committal to an institution. Under French law committal could only occur if a close relative
consented and to protect himself he tried to adopt Alan Searle as
his son. This involved him in a lawsuit with his daughter. His vast
public became aware that something was seriously wrong with their
hero. Where was the sorcerer? Where was the apprentice? Both
seemed to have been swallowed up by an enraged and vindictive
old man.

Then in 1962 a further bombshell, or rather series of detonations
week by week, burst in the pages of *The Sunday Express* and *Show*.
Maugham, it appeared, had been tempted by the offer of one
hundred thousand pounds from Lord Beaverbrook and an equivalent sum in dollars to let his autobiographical manuscript be
serialized. He painted a picture of his wife who had died in 1955
which made Hedda Gabler seem innocuous by comparison.
Maugham's close friends, Noël Coward and Beverley Nichols, and
others, simply could not believe their eyes as one appalling instalment
succeeded the next. Who would have thought the old man had so
much venom in him? Some of it was quite interesting, quite well
written. But really! All hell broke loose. If he could spill the beans,
so could they! Only they were going to have to wait until he was
dead. Books were written by various members of the Maugham
circle in eager anticipation of that event, revealing Maugham's
homosexuality and his doting upon Master Hacky.

What particularly shocked Noël Coward was the short shrift

Noël Coward as the writer, Hugo
Latymer, suggested in part by
Maugham, in *A Song at Twilight*, 1966,
with Lilli Palmer.

afforded to Haxton in *Looking Back*. He felt that Maugham could
have paid him a rather more gracious and candid tribute than the
following:

His death was a bitter grief to me. We had gone through a great deal
together. He had grave faults. He was a heavy drinker and a reckless
gambler. He had great merits. He had immense vitality. He was fearless.
He was always ready for an adventure and could turn his hand to anything, whether it was to persuade a stubborn car to behave reasonably
or in the wilderness to cook a savoury dinner.

Coward began to brood on what would happen if someone went
to Maugham and threatened to reveal to the world the true nature
of his relationship with this man and let his failed marriage be seen
by its lurid light. Then Coward read David Cecil's *Life of Max Beerbohm* and the account in it of a meeting in old age between Max
and his old love, the actress Constance Collier. The thought of this
confrontation gave him just the form he needed for a two-act play
with a Maugham-figure under threat from his former mistress to
have letters from his boyfriend published. He called it *A Song At
Twilight* (it was the first play in his final trilogy *Suite in Three Keys*)
and he played the part of Hugo Latymer himself.

In reality there weren't any letters because they had all been
burnt. Maugham spent his final years covering his tracks. In 1958
he and Alan Searle had a series of 'bonfire nights' in which they
systematically destroyed a heap of correspondence and manuscript
material, including the fourteen unpublished Ashenden stories. It
saddened Searle deeply to see it all go and on one occasion he kept
some especially precious documents back. Maugham came down to
breakfast in a very chirpy mood the next morning. He rubbed his
hands and said: 'That was a good night's work. Now we'll burn
everything you've hidden under the s-s-s-ofa.' Meanwhile he
requested his friends to burn his letters to them and instructed his
executors to forbid any of them from ever being published. The
only version of his life he wanted to appear after his death was the
Maugham version. Up to now he has been successful.

At the beginning of the 1960s people were wondering whether
Maugham was not indeed some sorcerer who had mastered the
secret of living for ever. At least they thought he might be the first
famous English author to publish a book on his hundredth birthday.
But by his ninetieth it was clear that the end could not be far distant.
In December 1965, a few weeks short of his ninety-second birthday,
he was taken, seriously ill, to the British American Hospital in Nice.

OPPOSITE
Cecil Beaton's portrait of Maugham at eighty-eight. 'An author', Maugham said 'will lead a life of inexhaustible interest and enjoy, as few can in this world today, the inestimable pleasure of freedom.'

When it became clear that nothing could be done to save him he was taken back to the Mauresque where he died in his own room, his mother's photograph by his bed, on 15 December. At prayers in The King's School on the following morning they stood in silence remembering in gratitude his life and work. His body was cremated and his ashes flown back to Canterbury where on 22 December in accordance with his wish, and in the presence of his daughter, Lady Glendevon, the Dean and the Headmaster, the ashes of William Somerset Maugham were interred in a plot of land adjacent to the Maugham Library. By then it was the Christmas holidays but some thirty boys returned for the ceremony in their school uniforms to form a respectful semi-circle around the more eminent mourners.

Notes on Sources

I have avoided identifying the source of quotations or information with index numbers. The titles and authors of sources have usually been incorporated into the text. However for the reader who wishes to pursue aspects of the subject in more detail I give below a list of my main sources in the order in which they occur.

1 From Embassy to Vicarage
British Embassy as birthplace: *The Paris Embassy* by Cynthia Gladwyn; Collins, 1977.
Maugham family history: *Somerset and all the Maughams* by Robin Maugham; Longman and Heinemann, 1966.
Maughams in Paris: *A Childhood in Paris* by Violet Hammersley in *Orpheus 2* edited by John Lehmann; John Lehmann, 1949.
Sarah Bernhardt: *Looking Back* by Somerset Maugham; *The Sunday Express*, 9 September 1962.
Dickens's trauma: 'Charles Dickens and David Copperfield' in *Ten Novels and Their Authors*; Heinemann, 1954.
Notebook inscription: Robin Maugham *op. cit*.
Sibert Saunders: 'Two Kent Authors' in *A Fourth Kentish Patchwork* by Robert H. Goodsall; Stedhill Publications, 1974.

2 The Black Book and Ibsen
The King's School: Robert H. Goodsall *op. cit*; *Schola Regia Cantauriensis: A History of Canterbury School Commonly Called the King's School* by C.E Woodruff and H. J. Cape; Mitchell Hughes and Clarke, 1908.
Heidelberg: *Looking Back*, 16 September 1962.
Ellingham Brooks: *Between Me and Life: a biography of Romaine Brooks* by Meryle Secrest; Maconald and Janes, 1976.
T. Fisher Unwin: *The Publishing Unwins* by Philip Unwin; Heinemann, 1972.
'A Lambeth Idyll': MSS of *Liza of Lambeth* in Maugham Library at The King's School, Canterbury.
Capri: *My Life and Times. Octave Four* by Compton Mackenzie; Chatto and Windus, 1965.

3 In and Out of Medicine
London years: *The Summing Up* and *Looking Back*.
Mrs Steevens at Merton Abbey: Preface by WSM to *What a Life!* by Doris Arthur-Jones; Jarrolds, 1932.
Maugham reviews Gissing: discovered by Pierre Coustillas of the University of Lille to whom I am indebted for a copy of the text.
Harry at first night: Robin Maugham *op. cit*.

4 Golden Sovereigns
Friendship with Kelly: *For Love of Painting: The Life of Sir Gerald Kelly KCVO PRA* by Derek Hudson; Peter Davies, 1975.

Tea with Arnold Bennett: *Journals* by Arnold Bennett edited by Newman Flower; Cassell, 1932–33.
Le Chat Blanc: 'A Fragment of Autobiography' by WSM, preface to 1956 re-print of *The Magician*, Heinemann; *Old Friends: Personal Recollections* by Clive Bell (who says he never met Maugham at this period); Chatto and Windus, 1971.
O'Conor and others: 'An Irishman in Paris' by Denys Sutton; *Studio* Vol. CLX 1960.
Aleister Crowley: *The Great Beast: The Life and Magick of Aleister Crowley* by John Symonds; Macdonald, 1971.
Struggling playwright: *Whatever Goes Up: The Hazards and Fortunes of a Born Gambler* by George C. Tyler; Bobbs-Merrill, 1924.
Lady Frederick produced: Preface to *The Plays of W. Somerset Maugham* Vol. I 1931.
'England's dramatist': *Punch*, 24 June 1908.
Drawing-room naturalism: *The Truth at Last* from Charles Hawtrey. Edited and with an introduction by W. Somerset Maugham; Thornton Butterworth, 1924.
Success, effect of: 1908 in *A Writer's Notebook*; Heinemann, 1949.

5 Jester into Spy
Affair with Sue and approach to Churchill: *Looking Back*, *The Sunday Express*, 23 September 1962.
Syrie's lover: *Selfridge: a biography* by Reginald Pound; Heinemann, 1960.
Wounds: *A Writer's Notebook*, 1914.
Proofs of *Of Human Bondage*: 'William Somerset Maugham: The English Maupassant – An Appreciation' by Desmond MacCarthy; Nash's Pall Mall Magazine, May 1933.

6 Eden and After
Brooke on South Seas: *Rupert Brooke a biography* by Christopher Hassall; Faber and Faber, 1964.
Material for 'Rain' and Gauguin trail: *A Writer's Notebook*, 1916; *The Two Worlds of Somerset Maugham* by Wilmon Menard; Sherbourne Press (Los Angeles), 1965.

7 Wiseman's Agent
William Wiseman: *British-American Relations 1917–1918: The Career of William Wiseman*; Princeton, 1969.
Czech nationalists: *Spy and Counter-Spy* by Will Irwin and Emanuel V. Voska; Harrap, 1941.
Official documents relating to Maugham's mission are printed by Robert Lorin Calder in *Somerset Maugham and the Quest for Freedom*; Heinemann, 1972.
Coolness at Embassy: *Looking Back*, *The Sunday Express*, 7 October 1972.

Kerensky and Savinkov: *A Writer's Notebook*, 1917.
Jack Straw in Russian: *Twenty-Five* by Beverley Nichols; Jonathan Cape, 1926.

8 East of Suez
Katherine Mansfield on *The Moon and Sixpence*: 'Inarticulations' *Athenaeum*, 9 May 1919, reprinted *Novels and Novelists* edited by J. Middleton Murry; Alfred A. Knopf, 1930.
Memories by Fay Compton, Harold Acton: broadcast in *The Faces of Maugham*: a radio portrait compiled and narrated by Anthony Curtis (BBC Radio 3), 25 January 1974.
Syrie v. Gerald: *A Case of Human Bondage* by Beverley Nichols; Secker and Warburg, 1966.
Real life source for *The Letter*: 'How murder on the veranda inspired Somerset Maugham' by Norman Sherry. *The Observer Colour Magazine*, 22 February 1976; *The Memoirs of a Malayan Official* by Victor Purcell; Cassell, 1965.
Cyril Connolly: *The Modern Movement: 100 Key Books from England, France and America*; André Deutsch/Hamish Hamilton, 1965.

9 The Villa Mauresque
Mauresque memories by Kenneth Clark, George Rylands, Frank Swinnerton: in *The Faces of Maugham*; Frederick Raphael: *Somerset Maugham and his World*; Thames and Hudson, 1977.
Lytton Strachey: quoted in *Lytton Strachey* by Michael Holroyd; Heinemann, 1967-8.
Virginia Woolf: *Diaries of Harold Nicolson* edited by Nigel Nicolson; Collins, 1966.
Lawrence on Ashenden: *Vogue*, 20 July 1928 reprinted *D.H. Lawrence Selected Literary Criticism* edited by Anthony Beal; Heinemann, 1955.
Rebecca West: 'Notes on Novels' *New Statesman*, 5 November 1921.
Sue as model for Rosie: this identification was first made by Robert Lorin Calder, *op. cit.*

10 His House in Order
Harry Gann as original of Lord George: Goodsall *op. cit.*
Walpole's reaction: quoted by Rupert Hart-Davis in his *Hugh Walpole: A Portrait of A Man, An Epoch and a Society*; Hart-Davis, 1952.
A.S. Frere: in *The Faces of Maugham*.
Elinor Mordaunt: as Toole Stott explains in his Bibliography, *Gin and Bitters. A Riposte* was the title of the anonymous American edition. The title of the English edition published, but then withdrawn, by Martin Secker in 1931 was *Full Circle* under the author's name. In showing me a copy of this rare item, Mr Secker said that 'Fredie' Maugham, the Lord Chancellor, told him, 'Willie would never have gone into the witness-box with that stammer of his.'
Ormond's accident: Robin Maugham, *op. cit.*

Rattigan on *Sheppey*: *The Faces of Maugham*.
Arthur Marshall and Lady Kelly on Haxton: *ibid*.
'The Saint': *Points of View*, Heinemann, 1958.
MacCarthy reviews *The Summing-Up*: An Artist Examines His Conscience' by Desmond MacCarthy *The Sunday Times*, 9 January 1938, and 'Mr Maugham and The Highbrows' *The Sunday Times*, 16 January 1938.

11 World War Two
Escape from France: serialized in four instalments in *The Saturday Evening Post* in March and April 1941; afterwards published in book form as *Strictly Personal*; Heinemann, 1942.
Short story anthology: *Tellers of Tales: 100 Short Stories from the United States, England, France, Russia and Germany*. Selected and With An Introduction by W. Somerset Maugham; Doubleday, Doran and Co. Inc. New York, 1939.
Maugham in America: *Sunshine and Shadow* by Cecil Roberts, Hodder and Stoughton, 1972.
Letter to Eddie Marsh: Berg Collection, New York Public Library, quoted by Toole Stott in *A Bibliography of the Works of Somerset Maugham*, 1973.
Dinner-party with René Clair: Garson Kanin, *op. cit.*
Diana Trilling on *The Razor's Edge*: 'Fiction in Review', *Nation*, 6 May 1944.
Cyril Connolly on above: 'The Art of Being Good', *New Statesman and Nation*, 26 August 1944.
A.S. Frere: *The Faces of Maugham*.
Roberts on Haxton's death: Cecil Roberts, *op. cit.*
Maugham's filmscript: *On Cukor* by Gavin Lambert. W.H. Allen, 1972.
Text of Speech: *Of Human Bondage: An Address* by W.S.M. designed and printed for the Library of Congress at the U.S. Government Printing Office, April 1946.

12 Vagrant Moods
'The Colonel's Lady' note: Garson Kanin *op. cit.*
Homage from Japanese: Francis King in *The Faces of Maugham*.
Kelly's Presidency and the Academy Dinner: Derek Hudson, *op. cit.* (There is a full recording of Maugham's Academy speech in the BBC Sound Archive.)
Maugham as Governor of The King's School: *F.J. Shirley an Extraordinary Headmaster* by David L. Edwards, S.P.C.K., 1969; *The Cantuarian*, December 1948.
India lost by Public Schools: *The Memoirs of Aga Khan*. Foreword by W.S.M.; Cassell, 1954.
Edmund Wilson attacks Maugham: 'Somerset Maugham and an Antidote' *New Yorker*, 8 June 1946, reprinted as 'The Apotheosis of Somerset Maugham' in *Classics and Commercials*; Farrar, Strauss, 1950.
Genesis of *A Song at Twilight*: life of Noël Coward by Cole Lesley; Jonathan Cape, 1976. Also Sheridan Morley in *The Faces of Maugham*.

Bibliography

A complete list of all the writings about Maugham does itself fill a book. Below are merely some suggestions for further reading.

Bibliographies
A Bibliography of the Works of W. Somerset Maugham by Raymond Toole Stott. Kaye & Ward. 1973.
Theatrical Companion to Maugham by Raymond Mander and Joe Mitchenson. Rockliff. 1955.
W. Somerset Maugham: An Annotated Bibliography of Writings About Him compiled and edited by Charles Sanders. Northern Illinois University Press. 1970.

Biographical and Critical
Somerset and all the Maughams by Robin Maugham. Longman and Heinemann. 1966.
Remembering Mr Maugham by Garson Kanin. Hamish Hamilton, 1966.
Somerset Maugham: A Guide by Laurence Brander. Oliver & Boyd. 1963.
Somerset Maugham: a biographical and critical study by Richard Cordell. Heinemann. 1961.
The Two Worlds of Somerset Maugham by Wilmon Menard. Sherbourne Press, Los Angeles. 1965.
The Pattern of Maugham by Anthony Curtis. Hamish Hamilton. 1974.
W. Somerset Maugham and the Quest for Freedom by Robert Lorin Calder. Heinemann. 1972.
Somerset Maugham and his world by Frederic Raphael. Thames & Hudson. 1977.

Bibliography of Maugham's Main Works

Maugham's works are published in hardback in the UK by Heinemann and in the US by Doubleday.

Novels
Liza of Lambeth 1897
The Making of a Saint 1898
The Hero 1901
Mrs Craddock 1902
The Merry-Go-Round 1904
The Explorer 1908
The Magician 1908
Of Human Bondage 1915
The Moon and Sixpence 1919
The Painted Veil 1925
Cakes And Ale 1930
The Narrow Corner 1932
Theatre 1937
Christmas Holiday 1939
Up at the Villa 1941
The Razor's Edge 1944
Then and Now 1946
Catalina 1948

Short stories
Orientations 1899
The Trembling of a Leaf 1921
The Casuarina Tree 1926
Ashenden 1928
Six Stories Written In The First Person Singular 1931
Ah King 1933
Cosmopolitans 1936
The Mixture As Before 1940
Creatures of Circumstance 1947
The Complete Short Stories of W. Somerset Maugham 1951
Seventeen Lost Stories 1969 (Published by Doubleday only in the US, contains contents of *Orientations* and other early stories Maugham excluded from the collected volumes)

Travel, Memoirs, Essays
The Land of the Blessed Virgin 1905
On a Chinese Screen 1922
The Gentleman in the Parlour 1930
Don Fernando 1935

The Summing Up 1938
France At War 1940
Books And You 1940
Strictly Personal 1941
Ten Novels and their Authors 1954
A Writer's Notebook 1949
The Vagrant Mood 1952
Points of View 1958
Purely For My Pleasure 1962
Looking Back 1962 (serialized in *Show* and *The Sunday Express* but not yet published in book form)

Plays
Dates are those of first production in England; * excluded by Maugham from the collected edition of his plays
*A Man of Honour** 1903
Lady Frederick 1907
Jack Straw 1908
Mrs Dot 1908
*The Explorer** 1908
Penelope 1909
Smith 1910
*The Tenth Man** 1910
*Grace** 1910
*Loaves and Fishes** 1911
The Land of Promise 1914
Caroline 1916
Caesar's Wife 1919
Home and Beauty (called in US *Too Many Husbands*) 1919
The Unknown 1920
The Circle 1921
East of Suez 1922
Our Betters 1923
The Constant Wife 1926
*The Letter** 1927
The Sacred Flame 1929
The Breadwinner 1930
For Services Rendered 1932
Sheppey 1933
*The Road Uphill** (Unproduced and unpublished)
The Plays of W. Somerset Maugham (Published in a collected edition for the first time in six volumes between 1931 and 1934 with prefaces on the art of playwriting, and now available in three volumes)

Index